The Ankole Kingship Controversy
Regalia Galore Revisited

Martin R. Doornbos

Fountain Publishers

First published as *Regalia Galore: The Decline and Eclipse of Ankole Kingship* in 1975 by East African Literature Bureau.

Fountain Publishers Ltd
P.O. Box 488
Kampala, Uganda
E-mail:fountain@starcom.co.ug
Website:www.fountainpublishers.com

Distributed in Europe, North America and Australia by African Books Collective (ABC), The Jam Factory, 27 Park End St., Oxford OX1 IHU, United Kingdom.
Tel: 44 (0) 1865-72686, Fax:1865-793298

© Martin R. Doornbos 2001
Revised edition 2001

All rights reserved. No part of this publication may be reproduced, stored in a retrieval system or transmitted in any form or by any means electronic, mechanical, photocopying, recording or otherwise without the prior written permission of the publisher.

ISBN 9970 02 281 4

1 2 3 4 5 05 04 03 02 01

Cataloguing-in-Publication Data

Doornbos, Martin R.
The Ankole Kingship Controversy: regalia galore revisited – Kampala: Fountain Publishers, 2001.
    p. cm

ISBN 9970 02 281 4
1. Monarchies – Uganda   2. Kingship (Ankole) – Uganda
  321.60'096761 – dc 20

Contents

	Preface	v
	Introduction	ix
1.	**The End as the Beginning**	1
2.	**Nkore and the Interlacustrine Area**	6
	The historical context of Nkore kingship	11
	The apparent paradox	14
	The limits of power of Nkore kingship	20
3.	**Incorporation and Expansion**	28
	Ankole and the Uganda context	30
	Ankole's expansion in scale	34
	The reduction of Bahinda influence	36
4.	**The Redefinition of Kingship**	42
	Perceptions of role conflict	50
	Colonial transformations and orientations towards kingship	53
5.	**The Neo-Traditionalisation of Ankole Kingship**	63
	The eclipse of the monarchy	69
	Symbolic exaltation and institutional relevance or decline: four configurations	74
6.	**Institutionalisation and Institutional Relevance**	81
	Ankole kingship in retrospect	83
7.	**The New Politics of Kingmaking**	91
	Background	92
	The western kingdoms	93
	The Ankole case	96
	Wider implications	99
	Conclusion	101

8.	**Epilogue: Regalia Galore Revisited**	**104**
	A way out of the stalemate	113
	Towards an Ankole museum of history and culture: A far-fetched proposition?	120
	Conclusion: A review of 'options'	121
	Appendix I	128
	Appendix II	130
	Appendix III	134
	Bibliography	137
	Index	140

Preface

It does not happen too often that interest in a particular book picks up some 25 years after its initial publication, long after its contemporaries have been shelved for good or more definitely re-cycled. Recently, this has been the case with *Regalia Galore: The Decline and Eclipse of Ankole Kingship,* which was first published in 1975 in Nairobi by the East African Literature Bureau on behalf of the East African Institute of Social Research (Makerere Institute of Social Research's predecessor). In recent years, the subject of this study has become topical again in light of the current political discourse in Uganda concerning the reintroduction of kingship in the southern and western parts of the country, particularly in Ankole.

In view of this interest, in February 2000 Fountain Publishers' James Tumusiime proposed to undertake the book's re-publication, in expanded and updated form. This provided me with a privileged opportunity to revisit the study, which I had first taken up in the 1960s during my time as a Research Fellow of the EAISR. A revisit to Uganda, allowing various discussions on the kingship restoration question and ready access to newspaper coverage of the dispute concerned, made this a manageable task. Accordingly, the present revised Fountain Publishers' edition, has been entitled *The Ankole Kingship Controversy: Regalia Galore Revisited.*

The reasons for a renewed interest in a study dealing with the historical background of Ankole kingship are not too difficult to discern. Along with the other monarchies in Uganda, the institution of kingship in Ankole was abolished in 1967 by President Milton Obotes's first government, amidst what then appeared to be a rather widespread indifference among the population of Ankole. In recent years, though, the future of Ankole kingship has become a highly contested issue, following attempts to restore the institution in the wake of the example of the reinstatement of the monarchy in neighbouring Buganda in 1993, and subsequently those of Toro and Bunyoro. In contrast, particularly to Buganda where the idea of kingship could count on broad popular support, social relations and perceptions of history in the Ankole region have rather appeared to militate against re-acceptance of monarchical institutions. In recent times, therefore, proponents and opponents of monarchical restoration have found themselves engaged in increasingly fierce verbal battles about the matter, in the Ugandan press, on the radio and television, in parliament and local councils, until it was left to rest in a provisional deadlock and stalemate from about April 2000 onwards. The proponents of restoration then announced they would pursue the matter again after the year 2003, when the 2001/2002 presidential, parliamentary and local councils elections will well be over.

Why did this question cause such controversy? The claims and counter-claims for and against restoration have been rather formidable, and the depth and complexity of arguments advanced from both sides increasingly added to the difficulty of finding a solution that might help defuse the issue. As both proponents and opponents consider the issue one of vital community interest, neither party could easily be found ready to give in and backtrack, a situation which basically obtains today. In the heat of debate, moreover, it is only to be expected that selectivity and perhaps a certain distortion of arguments will enter the picture, at times causing the dividing line between fact and fiction to get blurred. As kingship involves issues of identity which for some people can easily become sensitive one way or the other, there is a risk of community relationships getting seriously affected as the restoration issue lingers on. Yet the paradox now is that any clear-cut 'settlement' pro or con would be likely to leave one or another section of Ankole society disgruntled and embittered, with potentially adverse effects on social peace and security.

In Ankole, the problem is that in the former kingdom area, now consisting of the districts of Mbarara, Bushenyi and Ntungamo, the question of kingship does not stand by itself. It is widely perceived as having been intimately linked to a historical social structure internally split into two distinct ethnic sub-groups, Bahima (numerically a minority of pastoralist background) and Bairu (largely a peasant-cultivator community).Today Bairu largely identify themselves as Banyankore (the people of Ankole), though strictly that term should comprise Bahima as well as Bairu. While by and large the Bahima constituted the social and cultural milieu of Ankole kings, with the Bahinda clan (of the former Nkore kingdom) serving as their specific recruitment basis, Bairu in the past rather experienced the kingship as a symbol of ethnically defined subordination. The Bahinda themselves, though, had always considered themselves distinct from and 'above' both Bairu and Bahima.

Whereas that particular self-image may have had more ideological than social consequence, a division which certainly entailed significant political dimensions was the one which grew until well into the twentieth century between a politically powerful Bahima elite, on the one hand, and the Bairu majority as well as the larger numbers of common Bahima, on the other. In socio-economic terms, differences have been subsiding if not been obliterated: today there are rich and poor Bairu just as there are rich and poor Bahima. Culturally, however, the two Bahima groups continue to share a sense of common identity, as well as a special affection for the characteristic Ankole long-horn cattle (for some members of the Bahima elite increasingly a focus of weekend enjoyment on their ranches). As historically Bairu resentment of perceived ethnic superiority tended mainly to be directed towards the Bahima elite, due to a currently strong Bahima representation within senior army circles and in key government positions, there is some apprehension among Bairu about possible designs towards restoring a Bahima hegemony in Ankole.

In recent decades, ethnic friction between the two groups had its ups and downs, though throughout sentiments remained latently available to be mobilised around specific issues or disputes. In the years immediately after 1986, it first seemed as if the friction was markedly subsiding, partly as a result of the common context and social basis which the National Resistance Movement and its founder Yoweri Museveni had been promoting. With the issue of the restoration of Ankole kingship having been raised, however, this common ground now threatens to get lost, allowing old sores to re-surface. Hence the implications are much more pervasive, and potentially graver, than the question of the kingship by itself. There now appears to be an evident need to ensure that the rifts re-opened will not widen, but instead make room for a future that can promise social and human security for all.

Against the background of the current stalemate, it may be useful to reflect on the evolution of the institution now in dispute and review the historical trajectory and legacy of Ankole kingship. The present study perhaps has already gained some relevance towards the purpose, as the research for it was conducted long before the current crisis and might thus offer a more detached and independent perspective on the issue. Largely based on interviews and research data collected first during 1965-67, and in subsequent years till 1972, the book's original aim was to inquire into the circumstances that led to the transformations and decline to which the institution was subjected during colonial rule and the immediate years beyond. As its backflap read:

> This book explores the conditions under which the central institution of a traditional polity was eroded and came to lose its essential purpose. On the basis of extensive archival and other data, an analysis is made of the forces and processes by which the colonial order in Uganda radically restructured the position of the monarchy in Ankole society, reducing it to a faint reflection of its historical role and in the end to a redundant institution. Examining the underlying societal and organisational changes leading to this development, from pre-colonial days to 1967, the book tries to resolve a prime facie paradox: a proliferation of monarchical symbolism right up to the early years of Ugandan independence, followed by widespread indifference to the abolition of kingship.

Over and beyond these original objectives, the present text also aims at assessing the discourse on Ankole kingship as it has evolved since the restoration issue was tabled.

This Fountain edition thus starts out from the original text of *Regalia Galore*, with only a somewhat dated part of a theoretical discussion dropped in Chapter 6 and a new section added in Chapter 5. The latter juxtaposes the Ankole monarchy's neo-traditionalisation with some contrasted configurations of symbolic exaltation and institutional roles, and is drawn from a contribution to a symposium on *Development and Decline: The Evaluation of Sociopolitical Organization,* edited by Henri Claessen *et al* (1985). The core text is followed by a new chapter (7) on *The New Politics of Kingmaking,* discussing the kingship issue as it re-emerged after 1993. This additional chapter, co-authored with Frederick Mwesigye, was published earlier by Fountain Publishers in *From Chaos to Order: The Politics of Constitution-making in Uganda,* edited by Holger Bernt Hansen and Michael Twaddle (1995).

The book concludes with a fresh Epilogue, reflecting on the current stalemate around the restoration of Ankole kingship and the wider social and political implications of the Obugabe issue as well as revisiting the premises and interpretation of the original analysis in *Regalia Galore.* Finally, the Epilogue reviews various competin 'options' open or proposed to get out of the current stalemate around the restoration issue and itself advances one possible way of deflating the issue.

In revisiting the text, I have benefited greatly from the thoughtful comments of Godfrey Asiimwe, the Rev. Bishop Y. Bamunoba and Justus Mugaju. My greatest debt remains with Dr Tibamanya mwene Mushanga who introduced me to Ankole society and the sociopolitical dynamics that keep it together as well as divided.

Martin R. Doornbos
The Hague/Mbarara,
December 2000

Introduction

In much of the literature of public administration, sociology and political science a favourite theme is institutionalisation: if public bodies are to function effectively, or at all, they must be institutionalised. To become institutionalised, it is argued, political structures or administrative organisations must be accepted and legitimised in terms of the norms and values of a society. How exactly the chemistry of these 'norms and values' works is not entirely clear, but it is agreed that a smooth routine of political and administrative practices should ideally evolve.

There has also been a concern with institutions from another angle, namely, within those branches of anthropology and adjacent fields for which traditional authority has stood as a focal point. Here, too, the key to the functioning – and understanding – of institutions has long been held to lie within complex configurations of social values, belief-systems and cultural norms, if not in even more mystical properties. Again, if the norms and values appear supportive of an institution, social legitimation and institutional continuity are expected to obtain – the hallmarks of institutionalisation.

Of these two themes, the one evidently begins where the other ends. While one is primarily directed towards an understanding of inherited institutions, the other's orientation is essentially innovative, focusing on future institutions. Nonetheless, they share at least two major premises. One is the existence of, or movement towards, sociocultural congruence of the institution with its environment. The other, an in-built norm, is institutional longevity. The sum total of these qualities is institutional legitimisation.

It follows that a premium is ordinarily attached to the continued functioning of public institutions. Indeed, institutionalisation in such a sense has at times been equated with political development, the highest award of present day political science. But it also follows that questions are likely to be raised, and concern expressed, when institutional continuities are ruptured – through overthrow, abolition, or other means.

Here, then, is something of a dilemma. Normatively, institutions are expected to last, but evidently they often fail to do so. Instead, in a world of change, numerous situations show institutional rupture rather than continuity, and disjointedness rather than congruence. Are any such situations to be regarded as problematic?

To reverse Montesquieu, and to assert that any institution that breaks down suffers the fate it deserves, appears *prima facie* just as gross a generalisation as to say that all institutions should be maintained or maintain themselves. Nonetheless, in view of many incongruous situations in today's world, it may well be worthwhile to reconsider some of the normative implications of scholarly themes which converge in a concern with institutionalisation and institutional maintenance. But it also seems plain that these issues cannot be addressed without prior regard for the context in which the institutions operate.

Sociopolitical contexts are infinitely varied and changeable and conditions pertaining to one can hardly be expected precisely to apply to another. The abolition of the Ankole monarchy reported in this book also needs, in the first place, to be understood within its own specific context – which certainly was not 'typical'. But then, no conceivable example is 'typical'. To delve into one concrete case, therefore, suggests itself as a logical, if not necessary, first step towards formulating questions on the conditions under which an institution's termination might or might not be considered 'legitimate'.

This book is concerned with the processes which caused the decline and eclipse of a once meaningful institution, Ankole kingship. It resulted from a wider study of processes of change in Ankole society beginning in colonial times. These changes inevitably impinged upon Ankole's most distinctive institution, its kingship, making it pertinent to try to analyse their impact. Taking its departure from the abolition of the monarchy in 1967, this book first interprets the role of kingship in the pre-colonial era. On that basis, major contextual changes and developments during Uganda's colonial and post-colonial periods are traced in an attempt to understand popular reaction – or lack of it – to the abolition of kingship. The issue of institutional relevance is subsequently restated in more general terms.

A study of this kind must rely on various sources of information – archives, published records, oral tradition, and the relevant literature on the subject – which need to be reinterpreted and placed in a new framework before specific questions can be answered. Such a procedure may well give the presented data a somewhat novel appearance to readers familiar with the Ankole area. The author is well aware of this, as he is also of his status of non-Munyankore and non-Ugandan and the effects this may have on his perception. These considerations are no less significant given the rather delicate nature of a subject such as kingship. Recently, in fact, the possibility of restoring kingships has been a topic of public discussion in the changed political climate in Uganda; what is now basically a non-political subject might conceivably re-emerge as a controversial issue.

Still, if, from a distant observation point, certain structural trends and implications have been illuminated which are less readily recognised from a more immediate perspective and involvement, the purpose of this book will have been achieved. Moreover, this would constitute a modest repayment for the extensive support I have received from many quarters during its preparation. Many people have generously shared their time and insights with me and on many occasions have extended to me the hospitality for which Ankole is so rightly renowned. Though they remain unnamed here, they will doubtless recognise the considerable debt I owe them.

I am grateful to the Uganda Ministry of Regional Administrations and the District Commissioner, Ankole, for kindly allowing me to peruse archive materials relevant to the subject; to the Makerere Institute of Social Research for enabling me to engage in this research while I was a Fellow of the Institute; to the Institute of Social Studies, The Hague, for the time and facilities granted to write up this study. The responsibility for any views stated herein, however, is entirely my own.

M.R. Doornbos
The Hague, July 1973

Contemporary Ankole

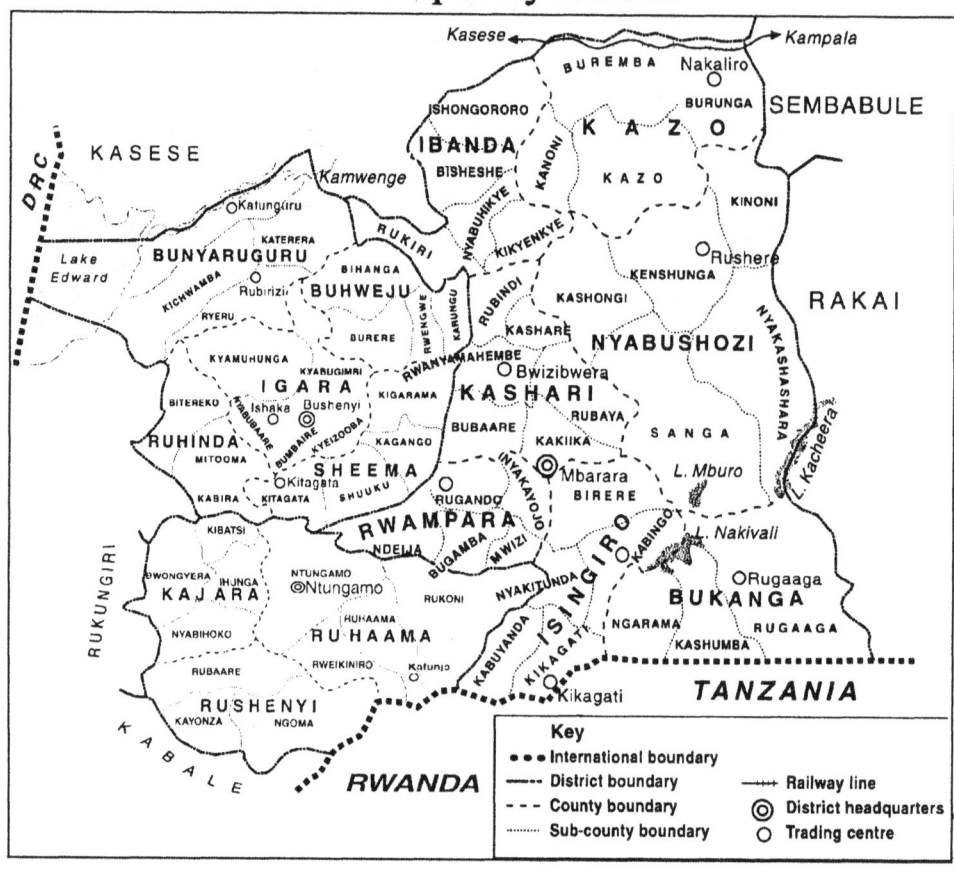

1
The End as the Beginning

Last Days of a Kingdom

The extinction of Ankole Federal and Kingdom Government was symbolised when the District Commissioner, Mr. Edward L. Athiyo, assumed all the administrative powers in the District. Accompanied by the former Kihimba (now known as the Administrative Secretary), Mr. Francis X. Tibayungwa, and the District Community Development Officer, Mr. Sam R. Kenyi, Mr. Athiyo handed a document to the former Omugabe, Sir Charles Godfrey Gasyonga, requesting him to vacate his palace by October 5. The official ceremonial articles, which included robes, crowns, Bagyendanwa drum and other royal drums were removed from Kamukuzi.

The former Omugabe's throne in the Eishengyero hall and in the church were also removed. The only (sic) in the Eishengyero hall was replaced by a chairman's seat. The official robes, necklaces and gloves for the former Omwigarire were also removed. This is in conformity with the new Constitution of the Republic of Uganda. The District Commissioner and the Administrative Secretary will be in charge of the District Administration until such time when a Secretary-General and his assistant will be elected. All the chiefs in Ankole have been advised when writing to the head of Ankole District Administration to address their letters to the Administrative Secretary and not to the Kihimba.

The Bishop of Ankole, the Rt. Rev. Kosea N. Shalita, arranged and conducted two special one-hour church services at St. James' Cathedral, Ruharo, near Mbarara, to bid farewell to the former Omugabe, Enganzi and the former Ministers.

The Eishengyero has been summoned to meet today to elect a chairman and his deputy and to choose five names to be sent to the Minister of Regional Administrations to declare a Secretary-General and his assistant.

From the **Uganda Argus** *28 September 1967*

Kingship in Ankole was formally abolished on 8 September 1967, following the ratification by the parliament of Uganda of a new constitution which proclaimed a unitary and republican form of government for the whole of Uganda. Together with the kingdoms of Buganda, Bunyoro and Toro, Ankole lost its semi-federal and monarchical status and henceforth was relegated to the rank of a district of Uganda.[1] Administrative offices and other institutions reminiscent of Ankole's monarchical heritage were disbanded or restyled in accordance with the pattern followed elsewhere in the country. Letterheads and placards bearing the name 'Ankole Kingdom Government' were altered with remarkable speed and instructions were issued concerning the proper way of addressing the new district officials. The king (Omugabe), Rubambansi Sir Charles Godfrey Gasyonga II, was given a month's notice to vacate his palace. And when, at the end of September 1967, Ankole's royal drum, Bagyendanwa, was unceremoniously loaded onto a lorry to be taken to storage in a government warehouse, the last major visible attribute of Ankole kingship was officially consigned to oblivion.

These few events marked the end of an epoch whose origins lay hidden in the past. It is generally assumed that the roots of Ankole[2] kingship date back at least four or five hundred years. In common with other interlacustrine kingdoms, it presumably owed its mythical charter to the semi-legendary Bacwezi, yet it is possible that a state structure existed in the Ankole area even before the alleged sojourn of Bacwezi on earth.[3] At any rate, legend and lore connected with kingship had lingered on from olden days till the present, and protocol and precedence remained matters of concern virtually till the last moment of monarchy.

Given the historical claims of the Ankole monarchy, it would be quite reasonable to expect its termination to signify a profoundly emotional clash of values. After all, few things are more powerfully symbolic of corporate existence than kingship itself. Kingship has often been the object of deeply affective values and in many instances has played a crucial role in shaping common political identities. Removing this capstone from a political structure might well leave an emotional vacuum not easily filled by alternative secular symbols. On the surface, the abolition of Ankole kingship would seem just another illustration of these conditions.

In fact, however, the operation did not carry such momentous implications. Naturally, most Banyankore engaged in lively discussion over the issue. But more significant than the display of interest as such was the nature of attitudes in Ankole. While these varied from group to group, there was clearly no general expression of regret. In June 1967, the first announcement of the proposed termination of kingship was made. Among the opinions then expressed, some clearly suggested that the changes would upset Ankole. And, as a matter of fact, some people were upset. Others, however, did not hesitate to express their satisfaction over the fall of the monarchy, and one especially vocal group immediately staged celebrations in Mbarara, the district capital.

Nonetheless, both rejoicing and regret were, on the whole, atypical reactions, as a much larger part of the population appeared basically indifferent to the outcome of the matter. For this wider segment, it made little difference whether there was an Omugabe or not, as life would presumably go on much as before. Theirs was often a reasoning based on quite pragmatic grounds, largely devoid of emotive responses. Many people, for instance, argued that since the Omugabe was no more than a figurehead neither his presence nor the office itself were of much consequence. Pros and cons were also formulated on utilitarian grounds, or on considerations of prestige. Preference for abolition, for instance, was not seldom argued in financial terms, since many Banyankore considered the money used for the upkeep of the monarchy to be unnecessary if not wasteful expenditure. Again, if a nostalgia for kingship was expressed at all, this was often not so much founded on any intrinsic merits, but rather on the idea that it had given Ankole more status and dignity than, for instance, the districts of northern Uganda.[4]

Few of these views fit the stereotyped notion of a traditional people intensely devoted to their overlord. Even the circles closest to the monarchy took the changes with remarkable detachment and restraint. The ministers of the Ankole kingdom government were obviously concerned about the loss of their titles and the perquisites they had enjoyed. But that seemed roughly the extent of their concern. As one commented privately, they cared little for either the person or the office of the Omugabe, but found the ministerial positions associated with Ankole's kingdom status quite gratifying. Another senior official, who was more intimately associated with the Omugabe, said that however much he personally deplored the termination of kingship, he had expected this to happen for the past twenty years and thus found reason to be thankful in the fact that it had lasted so long. The comment of the Omugabe himself was that if the government and the people found it fit that he should go, then he would do so. 'All that I am anxiously waiting for is an instruction from the Government on what to do next.'[5] Meanwhile, administrative officers who had been in the service of the Omugabe's government were dutifully engaged in obliterating the remaining vestiges of monarchism from the facade of the political system; the operation was smooth and unspectacular, as if it were merely a matter of disposing of an already superfluous appendage.

If one takes the view that affective loyalties are a necessary ingredient of kingship, then the behaviour of the Banyankore in 1967 may well have seemed inexplicable. Certainly, the argument that the people of Ankole refused to express their innermost feelings out of fear of punishment cannot withstand critical examination. Remarkably candid discussions had appeared in the press prior to the enactment of the 1967 constitution, followed up in the course of public debate, and whoever wished to publicly state his support of the monarchy had been quite free to do so.[6] Hence, the question remains as to why the Banyankore reacted so indifferently. Our assumption is that there is no reason to dispute the genuineness of the opinions expressed in Ankole, and indeed that there was a certain logic to these views. Thus, it suggests that in 1967 kingship had little meaning for the average Munyankore, either as a symbol or an institution. While there is no gainsaying that Ankole kingship served as a major focal point of political cohesiveness prior to the introduction of British rule, the effects of the transformations brought in the wake of colonisation appear to have made the institution increasingly redundant.

This study is concerned with this process and tries to account for the conditions which turned a once meaningful institution into a largely superfluous appendage of the Ankole political framework. In a general sense, its theme is familiar: incorporated into the Uganda political framework by the vagaries of colonial history, Ankole kingship faced many of the characteristic strains and stresses following European colonisation in Africa. What was traditionally the linchpin of the social system in this process was confronted with the demands of an entirely different organisational framework, that of a colonial administrative state. Under the impact of these new arrangements, Ankole provided one more instance of the puzzles and perplexities which have marked processes of colonial incorporation and adjustment of traditional patterns of authority.

Even though the effect of these changes had been to make the monarchy largely obsolete, its abolition ultimately resulted from a challenge to the integrity of the wider Uganda polity of which it formed part, a challenge, moreover, which originated from outside the Ankole subsystem. Nor is this the only factor that lends special interest to the Ankole case. That the abolition of the Ankole monarchy should have aroused few strong reactions is all the more intriguing considering the upheaval provoked under similar circumstances in Buganda. Part of the explanation lies in the processes of adjustment and interaction that have taken place over the years within Ankole as well as between Ankole and the Uganda-wide political system.

To better understand the relative ease with which the removal of the Ankole monarchy was effected we need to examine the structural transformations which over the years have affected the role of kingship in Ankole society. Rather than a one-to-one substitution of modern for traditional authority structures, the social, political and geographical contexts of the kingdom were transformed at the same time that the kingship itself was being restructured. At the turn of the century, when colonial rule was introduced, the formal boundaries of the kingdom underwent considerable expansion; these territorial gains were offset, however, by the political limitations arising from its incorporation into Uganda. From that point on, the very existence of the monarchy came to depend on policy considerations of an entirely different nature from what might have been the case had the kingdom been treated as a single political entity.

Moreover, various characteristics of the social structure of Ankole had a significant bearing on the changing role of kingship, in particular the ethnic division between Bairu and Bahima and the loss of influence suffered by the traditional ruling clan, the Bahinda. In the wake of colonisation new patterns of relationship emerged among groups, and these in turn gave rise to new perceptions of the role of kingship in the system. In brief, a rather complex set of factors must be taken into account if one is to appreciate the roots of this transformation. In order to understand how the redefinition of kingship affected the capacity of the institution to operate as a meaningful element in the political system, we will first consider the role of kingship in the precolonial society. We shall need to be particularly concerned with the social basis of power and the manner in which the functions of the state, here those of a traditional African kingdom, were structured and discharged. Against this background we will be better able to evaluate the changes that were brought to bear upon this society as a result of colonialism and understand the factors that eventually led to the decline and eclipse of the institution of kingship in Ankole.

Notes

1. Article 118 (1) of the 1967 Constitution of Republic of Uganda read :
   'The institution of King or Ruler of a Kingdom or Constitutional Head of a District, by whatever name called, existing immediately before the commencement of this Constitution under the law then in force, is hereby abolished.'
2. The name Ankole is a mixed Luganda-English corruption of Nkore, the pre-colonial kingdom around which the Ankole district was formed. In the discussion that follows 'Nkore' refers to the nineteenth century kingdom, 'Ankole' to the enlarged post-1900 kingdom-district and 'Ankole area' to the historical region comprising Nkore and its surrounding areas.
3. Z. C. K. Mungonya, 'The Bacwezi in Ankole', *Uganda Journal* XXII, I, 1958:18-21; and C. C. Wrigley, 'Some Thoughts on the Bacwezi', *Uganda Journal*, XXII, 1, 1958:11-17.
4. Audrey I. Richards (ed.), *East African Chiefs*, London, 1959:357-58.
5. *The People,* Kampala 17 June 1967.
6. See letters to the Editor in *The People* and *Uganda Argus*, June through September 1967. For an early expression of the monarchist minority viewpoint, consult the article 'Banyankore do not support the new Constitution' (translated title), *Sekanyola*, 10 May 1966.

2
Nkore and the Interlacustrine Area

For many centuries prior to British rule, the Ankole area had been politically and culturally related to various other societies in the interlacustrine region of eastern Africa. The kingdom of Nkore,[1] which was the nucleus around which the Ankole district was formed at the beginning of the colonial period, was centrally situated within this large region: its most important neighbours were Bunyoro-Kitara to the north, Karagwe and Buhaya to the south, Mpororo and Rwanda to the southwest, and Buganda to the east.[2] In a narrower circle around Nkore lay a string of smaller kingships, including Koki, Buzimba, Buhweju, Igara. Some key trade routes, travelled by Arabs and others (especially to the Katwe market and salt deposits), passed through the area.[3] Other contacts, notably political relationships, were maintained over long distances. Pastoralists on trek covered wide circles; warfare, droughts and epidemics at times caused groups to move and resettle within the region at large, or even further away. For these reasons, already, the interlacustrine region featured a certain unity and distinctiveness, some characteristics of which are still found today in Ankole and elsewhere.

Politically, the region constituted a kind of international arena *avant la lettre*. Within this area several distinct polities–some that would be called states (if not empires), others proto-states, some independent, others semi-independent by today's terminology– exercised powers and engaged in inter-state relationships. Reflected in shifting coalitions, tribute relationships and lines of conflict, their respective influence now grew, then subsided, to continuously form new balances of power.

For centuries, the major axis along which power extended and contracted lay roughly north-south between Bunyoro-Kitara-based Babito ruling groups, on the one hand, and the Bahinda originating from the Rwanda area on the other. At its zenith, Bunyoro-Kitara's suzerainty was claimed to reach far into the area that is today the Bukoba region of north-west Tanzania. Until well into the nineteenth century, the basic trend was for the Bahinda to gradually extend their control northwards into areas which had for long been subject to Babito overrule. Partly paralleling the decline of Bunyoro-Kitara's power as a result of these Bahinda encroachments, a third party ascendancy and expansion of Buganda was made possible during the nineteenth century.[4]

Thus, in the specific case of Nkore, its relative standing within this pattern was strongly dependent upon the role and pursuits of its more powerful neighbours and suzerains–Bunyoro-Kitara, Rwanda and, less directly,

Buganda. Roughly until the early part of the nineteenth century Nkore, though one of the Bahinda states, had been weaker than, if not actually dependent upon, Bunyoro-Kitara. With Bunyoro-Kitara's decline, Nkore's political position gradually became stronger. Several smaller neighbouring states, such as Igara, Buhweju and Buzimba, that had earlier been subject to Babito overrule, first became 'independent' (most notably in the case of Buhweju) and eventually were made to acknowledge Nkore's paramountcy, expressed through the tribute they paid to its ruler. Nkore's 'imperialism' finally reached a peak during the rule of Ntare V, shortly before the British arrived on the scene.

Culturally, manifold areas of overlap existed between the societies of the interlacustrine region.[5] With few exceptions their languages were all patterned on the basic Bantu structure. On top of this, several languages were especially closely related and, in some instances, two or more societies virtually shared a linguistic identity. Runyankore, for example, was basically identical to Rukiga spoken by the Bakiga (who originally lived in the present Kabale district of Uganda), so that in the present century a common orthography could be developed for the two languages.[6] While Runyankore was less close to Luganda, its linguistic affinities with, among others, Karagwe and Bunyoro-Kitara (and the latter's nineteenth-century offshoot Toro) easily allowed two-way communication with these societies. Pockets of linguistically distinct sub-areas nonetheless persisted in various parts, such as Bunyaruguru in the present Ankole area or the Bakonzo and Baamba parts of the Rwenzori region. But even in such instances what appeared to underscore the cultural ties within much of the interlacustrine region was the tendency for a certain give and take – of vocabulary if not of grammar – to permit a fair amount of linguistic assimilation, probably more than occurred later after the languages were codified.

Similar overlaps were salient in regard to other aspects of culture. Various interlacustrine societies, especially the Bahinda-ruled areas, had basically similar myths of origin, the common mythology being the presumed sojourn in the region of the semi-legendary Bacwezi.[7] Subsequent to that era, Bahinda rule itself became mythologised, though most groups nonetheless gave these myths their own, slightly different but yet unique, interpretation.

One such adaptation was the mythical charter predominant in the Ankole area. According to this, Ruhanga, the Creator, once put his three sons, Kakama, Kahima and Kairu, to a competitive test by entrusting each of them with the task of keeping a milkpot full of milk for one whole night. Kakama won and was charged with the rule of the country. Kahima, who had given some milk to Kakama, was made to look after the cattle, while Kairu, who had spilled his milk, was told to till the soil.[8]

More prosaically other similarities pertained to modes of existence and social relationships. Throughout most of the interlacustrine region, subsistence was based on one or another of a few main poles: agriculture, cattle-raising, some fishing – agriculture being mainly concentrated on beans, millet, cassava, plantains, or some combination of these.[9] (In the Ankole area millet and beans were historically the main crops; plantains spread largely after the coming of the first Baganda agents.[10]) Additional economic goods characteristic of the region included iron implements (e.g. spearheads, hoes, axes), salt, bark-cloth, pots, baskets and wooden vessels, augmented in the second half of the nineteenth century by ivory, arms and slaves.[11]

Again, social organisation followed a few basic patterns, its diversity being largely a question of variations on a theme. Residence patterns were generally based on scattered homesteads, not villages, a fact with far-reaching implications in terms of the kind of socio-political frameworks that evolved. Over and beyond the immediate extended family, clan membership – of either a corporate group or a reference category – was common throughout and of major importance.

For purposes of land utilisation and security, if for no other, it appears that clans used to be territorially more concentrated than they are at present. Today, in not a few instances only a historic place name identifies a clan with a particular locality. Mostly patrilineal and exogamous, as in Ankole,[12] though varying as to the criteria and nomenclature of identification (e.g. totem avoidance as a principle as opposed to or in conjunction with, accepted area of origin), it was also common for clan-sections to be ranked in terms of higher or lower status and for some of them to demonstrate over time a measure of vertical social mobility.[13]

Status differentials in other than clan terms were similarly pervasive in many parts of the region. Institutionalised in greater or lesser formal fashion, though with variations as to the exact behaviour expressive of hierarchical social relationships, in various areas inequality of status was particularly pronounced – socially, politically, economically. Among other things, these inequalities were closely related to patronage relationships, and to an occupational structure in which, for example, some people were cattle-keepers, others cultivators, blacksmiths, woodcarvers, potters and musicians.

Over and beyond these various political and cultural connections, two characteristics made the interlacustrine region particularly distinctive. One was the co-existence in many, though by no means all parts of the area, of two or more different ethnic groups, often in positions of unequal status vis-à-vis one another [14]. The other was the existence of institutions of kingship in various – again not all – societies within the region. The exact pattern of ethnic relationships, and monarchical powers varied from case to case. As regards ethnic relationships, variations depended, among other things, on the extent of social distance between the groups concerned, the occurrence and frequency of intermarriage among them, and the extent to which they were politically autonomous within the system as a whole. The latter again was closely connected to the extent of their involvement in a common system of economic relationships, as opposed to the pursuit of separate economic activities. As to the pattern of monarchical powers, variations corresponded with the degree of centralisation of the system, in conjunction with the weight of appointive as opposed to hereditary criteria of chiefly recruitments, and the existence or absence of a central administrative machinery as against sub-unit structures of authority.

In each case, it was therefore the particular combination of these two patterns, of ethnic status designations and the institutions of kingship, which defined the specific nature of political relationships in the interlacustrine society concerned. In Rwanda, for example, politically superior Batutsi and subordinate Bahutu were more integrated, through a system of clientship arrangements, into basically a unified political and economic system, than had evolved in various neighbouring societies. Intermarriage took place here, though not to the extent that it obliterated ethnic distinctions between the two groups or replaced these by status distinctions only. In Rwanda as elsewhere the kingship stood at the pinnacle of this pyramidal web of relationships[15]. In Bunyoro-Kitara and Toro, by contrast, assimilation between high-status Babito and Bahuma and low-status Bairu (of which the latter two were historically related to Nkore's Bahima and Bairu) had taken place to a degree where the respective terms had basically come to denote status, rather than ethnic distinctions. Politically and economically, these systems had also become more vertically integrated, though generally with Babito, Bahuma and Bairu placed in a descending order of prominence. Also – in the nineteenth century – due to the absence of strong central bureaucratic structures, there was a high potential for horizontal fragmentation separate units.[16]

Notwithstanding general similarities on account of the existence of kingship in conjunction with ethnic stratification (not to speak of other cultural ties), pre-colonial political relationships in Nkore differed in some significant respects from the patterns in both Rwanda and Bunyoro-Kitara and other interlacustrine societies. The Bairu-Bahima division, which in terms of ethnicity and status bears a certain, though not very close, resemblance to that between Batutsi and Bahutu in Rwanda, existed also in neighbouring systems such as Karagwe and Buhaya, but in few places had it remained as clearcut as in the case of Nkore.

Briefly, Bairu and Bahima lived in the same general area, though in various ways Bahima enjoyed more powers than Bairu did. The two groups were involved in a variety of social, political and economic contacts, and some flexibility in the general, somewhat diffuse, status system appears to have allowed a limited possibility of social mobility and in the long run even some minimal assimilation. Nonetheless, Bairu and Bahima by and large remained more distinct, ethnically as well as socially, and kept more exclusively engaged in different bases of subsistence than was true for most adjacent areas. Whereas their distinct modes of life and patterns of social interaction were contained within a general common context, there was a Bahima-oriented–and dominated – political system which, as reflected in its kingship, lacked not only the structure but in a sense also the focus and 'interest' to sustain a pervasive downward control. Thus, Nkore's complex political framework was characterised not only by separate economic pursuits of its ethnic groups, which were nonetheless combined with a pattern of subordination, but also by two 'levels' of state functions – differing in intensity, purposes and the nature of rewards and sanctions passed in relation to the two groups. Other lines of differentiation and authority qualify this pattern further. To see this, we will first briefly consider the background of Bairu-Bahima relationships, then discuss the institution of kingship itself.

A few reservations must however be mentioned. One is that the present discussion will primarily concern Nkore, not the other areas included into the expanded Ankole district. This is mainly because more extensive information is available on pre-colonial Nkore than on some of the other areas incorporated into Ankole.[17] Nkore constituted the largest and politically the most important society among those which made up the new district. Although roughly similar patterns existed in some of the annexed areas, especially those obtained from Mpororo, demographic and political changes which followed the redefinition of Ankole society at the beginning of colonial rule still do not permit a direct juxtaposition of socio-political patterns in pre-colonial Nkore with those in the new district.

Timewise, a second reservation is necessary. Our discussion will be partly based on oral evidence and on sources written in the early part of the last century, both of which presumably refer primarily to the immediately preceding period, i.e. the latter part of the nineteenth century.[18] A relative lack of evidence on historic processes makes it difficult to distinguish between the Nkore political system of one period and another: to do that would in any case lie outside the scope of this study[19]. Thus, our references to the pre-colonial period refer mainly to the latter part of the nineteenth century without implying that this period was in any way 'typical'. (In fact, there are reasons to assume that this period was not typical: that while Nkore was aggrandising, its potential for internal fissure became strongly enhanced; and that the prominence it nonetheless received as a nucleus for colonial state formation was largely due to the earlier experience of the British with the centralised system in Buganda and their belief that a similarly strong state organisation obtained in Nkore.)

Closely connected is a third and final caveat which, though in principle pertinent to most historical analysis, is certainly in order in the present case. In the virtual absence of first-hand, written information on pre-colonial Nkore, available evidence is largely confined to secondary source materials and the oral traditions and memories of elderly members of Ankole society. Both frequently pose similar problems of analysis – a certain inexplicitness on key questions, contradictory accounts and, at times, rather *a priori* interpretations which may be instigated by the present perspectives, political or otherwise, of observers or participants. One major, if not entirely foolproof, rule of thumb that can be employed in regard to any such ambiguities, is a cross-checking and critical re-analysis of the available data – a method on which this essay is largely based.

The historical context of Nkore kingship

Ankole's economy has been traditionally based on cattle and crops. Historically, the possession of cattle, especially breeding cattle, was limited to the Bahima who numerically formed a minority. Bahima life was very much centred around their famed long-horn cattle, which for them were not only a means of subsistence, but a symbol of wealth, power and prestige. The usual assumption has been that Bairu were not allowed to have cattle.[20] However, a more direct and simpler explanation appears to be that economically Bairu were not in a position, ordinarily, to obtain cattle, basically for lack of equivalent exchange value. The Bairu majority have traditionally been mainly engaged in agriculture. This historical division of labour still has contemporary relevance: at present most Bairu, even those who own cattle,[21] are primarily engaged in agriculture, whereas the majority of Bahima continue to be mainly occupied in cattle rearing.

It is not known exactly what proportions Bahima and Bairu represented within the population of pre-colonial Nkore. Nonetheless, it is beyond doubt that the number of Bahima was substantially larger than the 5-10 per cent which it is assumed they constitute in the present Ankole area[22]. One explanation for this relative decrease of the Bahima population in Ankole, as compared to Nkore, is the fact that most of the areas incorporated into what became Ankole district were more predominantly Bairu populated than was Nkore. Moreover, roughly parallel to this incorporation, i.e. the latter part of the nineteenth century and the beginning of the twentieth, rinderpest, other epidemics, and political conflict caused many Bahima to move away, into Buganda and further east, thus leading also to an absolute decrease of the Bahima population. It has been locally estimated that the Bahima constituted as much as 40-60 per cent of the population of precolonial Nkore, a figure which may well be somewhat inflated.[23] But while it is difficult to establish the proportions of Bahima and Bairu which obtained in Nkore with any great degree of accuracy, for an understanding of political power relationships in the precolonial society it must be kept in mind that the Bahima component was in any case considerably larger than it is at present.

According to a rather widely held assumption, the Bahima migrated into the present Ankole area some four or five centuries ago, and set up the state structures which have been handed down through time. This 'Hamitic myth' has been a dominant theme in explanations of the origins of the interlacustrine states virtually since Speke's account of his first explorations in the area.[24]

Debates around this theme continue today, with archaeologists, historians, and biochemists among the interested parties.[25] The conquest theories of state origins have recently been criticised as being based on prejudice. In the summary of C.P. Kottak, 'there has been a regrettable tendency...to assume that wherever sophisticated political developments have occurred in East Africa, they could not possibly have developed internally. They must either have been borrowed from some 'superior' group or have been imposed by conquerors of some sort. Whether Nilotes or 'Nilo-Hamites' conquering Bantu, or Cushites or Hamites conquering some indigenous population, the resulting picture has been the same – a dominant ruling class or caste of ultimately foreign origin, which somehow managed to form a state out of something that was not a state before.'[26]

Certainly, even if the Bahima came in from elsewhere – as still may well have been the case – to connect the establishment of state structures with the arrival of the Bahima essentially amounts to a twofold hypothesis, one for which the necessary evidence is lacking. On the contrary, while there would seem to be no *a priori* reason why two such developments should have coincided in the first place, the inauguration rites of the Omugabe of Nkore used to include some rather unpastoral ceremonies, such as the planting of millet seed, which might indicate the existence of kingship in an era even before the Bahima gained political control.[27] It seems possible, therefore, that what long used to be a Bahima-dominated state structure has been projected back into history to establish a claim on its origin. Meanwhile, on a mythological plane (as opposed to historical speculation), the Bahinda royal clan of Nkore supposedly had an origin which was distinct from that of both Bahima and Bairu.[28] But this again did not alter the fact that in known history, the Bahinda led essentially the same type of life as Bahima and have generally identified themselves with Bahima interests. The Bahinda have also normally been considered a Bahima clan, although a somewhat special one. Nkore might therefore well be called a Bahima state,[29] notwithstanding the references to the myth of origin which Bahinda and other Bahima often made (and make). The function of this myth was basically a legitimising one, as it purported to establish a statutory equality between Bahima and Bairu and might thus conceal the social distance between the latter two groups, even if (but precisely because) it recognised the supremacy of one section of the Bahima, the Bahinda.

Bairu and Bahima speak the same language, Runyankore, although with different accents and with various expressions and metaphors that are unfamiliar to members of the opposite group. The two groups are also linked through a common clan system, that is, Bairu and Bahima members of a clan recognise a common avoidance totem.[30] But their common clans are differently named by the Bairu and the Bahima segments and the rules of clan-exogamy adhered to by Bairu are not followed by Bahima.[31] Some clans have a more predominantly Bairu, others a more predominantly Bahima membership. But Kinyankore clans are essentially reference, not corporate groups, so that members normally do not know each other. Intermarriage between members of the two groups has been rare; in the past, according to recollections by Banyankore, the main – though limited – contact appears to have been that of Bahima taking Bairu 'concubines'.[32]

There is a good deal of evidence to suggest that Nkore was primarily a state of the Bahima, as well as for the Bahima, but that this hegemony was not necessarily, at least not fully, extended to other spheres of life. While some of the Bairu were directly subservient to Bahima, and while Bairu generally enjoyed some fewer rights and privileges than Bahima in the contact between the two groups, a major part of the Bairu definitely lived a fairly autonomous existence.[33] Even more certain is that the political life of the kingdom mostly revolved around matters that were virtually the exclusive concern of Bahima, such as warfare, cattle raising (and raiding), adjudication of disputes, and other related matters.[34] Hence, while some Bairu were expected to provide products and services to the Omugabe and other senior Bahima, and whereas at times the requisitions demanded from them may have been rather arbitrary, there is little indication of a pervasive and continuous political control exercised over all of them. Thus, if in a general sense Bairu have often been considered a 'subject' category, their lack of participation in the political process seems primarily explained by the characteristics of the 'Bahima state', which was especially geared to the requirements of pastoralism. The Ankole framework, therefore, basically comprised two distinct types or levels of political relationships. Between Bahima and Bairu relationships tended to be intermittent, though often based on unequal advantages. By comparison within the Bahima stratum the relationships that pertained to the state organisation were more frequent and intimate, and appear to have been roughly of the kind characteristically existing between 'freemen'.[35]

It was within this context, which juxtaposed a basically Bahima state framework with the Bairu communities, that the institution of Nkore kingship functioned and in fact stood as the pivot around which the affairs of the state revolved. It is already clear that the office of the Omugabe, while to many Bairu he undoubtedly was an ultimate symbol of power and, in principle, the supreme arbiter of conflicts among men,[36] in fact was quite far removed from day to day Bairu affairs. While the Omugabe clearly stood as the centrepiece of the Nkore political system and his position no doubt inspired considerable awe for many Bairu, the ties that linked them to him were not especially conducive to strong affective identification with the political system. For the Bahima, on the other hand, the Omugabe was the focal point of their political relationships. They certainly enjoyed a much more intimate relationship with him. He was closely involved in their affairs and he in fact often used to move camp with his cattle as other Bahima did. Moreover, not only was his way of life much the same as theirs, but he was also regarded as the protector of their interests. In the light of the ethnic division, therefore, the historical Nkore system differed fundamentally from, for instance, traditional Buganda with its more homogeneous population structure. Again, contrary to what its mythology would imply, traditional Nkore was not a system in which Bairu and Bahima were basically united in a mystical identification with its kingship. Instead, the institution of Nkore kingship must be understood within the context of the state system, which was primarily based on intra-Bahima relationships.

The apparent paradox

The analysis of Nkore kingship[37] appears complicated by a conceptual problem which is more often encountered in the study of historic African states. When glancing through the available literature, or talking to the reputedly knowledgeable members of such societies, one of the more persistent images presented shows the traditional ruler as holding absolute powers. Further queries, however, may well yield an entirely different picture. A consideration of the distribution of authoritative functions, or of the consultations, bargaining and conflicts involved in the political process, can suggest a far greater dispersal of power than might have been anticipated.[38]

Such an ambivalence of interpretations is characteristic of much of the literature on Nkore. On the one hand, the Omugabe figures as omnipotent and despotic, as a ruler who wields unlimited powers and who has an absolute, autocratic sway over his kingdom. On the other hand, he emerges as essentially a *primus inter pares*, a mediator between conflicting interests, and an instrument in the settlement of disputes. More intriguing still is that both images should sometimes coexist within the same source, leaving the reader at a loss to reconcile one with the other.[39]

When reviewing some of these images, we can find an 'absolutist' view of Nkore kingship stated quite strongly in the work of Roscoe, who wrote in 1923: 'The government of the country of Ankole was autocratic and the power was in the hands of the Mugabe or ruler, whose rule was absolute and his decision on any matter final.'[40] Furthermore, Roscoe asserted, 'The Mugabe had the power of life and death over all his subjects, and it was believed that his people held their property solely through his clemency, for he was the owner of all the land and all the cattle.'[41] This last point was re-emphasised in an official publication of 1938, which stated that 'The Omugabe laid claim to all the cattle in the country, being as much the ruler of cattle as he was of men. This claim, furthermore, was no idle one, for the Omugabe could and did take whatever cattle he wished from whomsoever he pleased...'[42] Two years later, in 1940, Oberg expressed himself in much the same vein: 'The position of the Mugabe was exalted, his authority supreme, his leadership all-embracing.' Oberg further concluded that 'Power...both physical and spiritual, was the inherent quality of kingship.'[43]

These views have been echoed virtually till the present day. For instance, in an essay prepared some years ago by the Ntare History Society it is claimed: 'Before the British brought in democracy (sic), the type of government which prevailed was...despotic. The king's powers were unlimited. He could, with a word, prevent or make a man's fortune.'[44] Another illustration is provided by Vansina. Having constructed a typology of African kingdoms on the basis of a scale of decreasing centralisation, i.e. ranging from the most centralised state structures on one end to federative arrangements (in which the king is 'only *primus inter pares*') on the other, Vansina goes on to characterise Nkore as a 'clear case' of the first type, namely a 'despotic kingdom' in which 'the king appoints all other officials and wields absolute power in practice and in theory.'[45]

These examples could be multiplied, but for our purposes they suffice to indicate one persistent trend of thought according to which the traditional monarchical institutions of Nkore were synonymous with those of a 'despotic' state. At the root of this misrepresentation lies a confusion between the actual and ideal aspects of authority vested in the Omugabe, which will be discussed below. But it should be noted that, on the face of it, there was much in the traditional political culture which seemed to support the idea. In monarchical ideology, the Omugabe was seen as possessing extraordinary and divine faculties, unequalled in other human beings. He was known, for instance, as *Rubambansi*, 'He who stretches the Earth',[46] which clearly stressed his omnipotence; as *Omukama* 'The Milker', again typifying him as the benefactor who supplied his people with their food; and as *Nyakusinga*, 'The Victorious', who overcomes all enemies.

Moreover, as Omugabe, 'The Divider' or 'The one who has been given authority',[47] he posed as the direct descendant of the Creator Ruhanga, which again exemplified his supernatural powers. In the ritual he engaged in and the ceremonial with which he was surrounded, these aspects were all symbolically expressed. On his accession, for instance, he would purify the country, and when disease came to the land he would curse it to dispel it. In the night, it was believed, he could not turn or he would turn his kingdom over.[48] Finally, tradition relates that the Omugabe could not die a natural death, but was obliged to take a poison when his powers began to fail him.[49] When this happened, the word for death was not used, but it was said that 'heaven has fallen' or 'fire has gone out'. Again, his body was not buried, but taken to a place where his spirit would reincarnate itself into a lion.

All these notions thus seem to underscore the supreme and exalted position of the Omugabe. In practice, however, the Omugabe's powers to impose his will were severely restricted.[50] A variety of groups and individuals participated in the making of decisions and their influence could not be easily circumvented by the Omugabe. We might first note here the position of the Omugabe's mother and sister, who were consulted on many issues and whose opinion, if only because of the closeness of their relationship to the Omugabe, carried no small amount of weight. But of special importance in this respect were the Bakungu or senior chiefs, who were responsible for territorial divisions and who also served as the Omugabe's counsellors. Decisions were discussed at great length in the assembly of these chiefs, usually until a consensus emerged which would then be articulated by the Omugabe. The duality of functions of the Bakungu had significant consequences, for it meant that the officials involved in formulating major decisions were also responsible for their implementation, while the Omugabe had no other administrative instrument to override their influence.[51]

Although the Bakungu were expected to spend a good deal of time paying court to the Omugabe, and while this obligation might conceivably have prevented them from asserting their independence from the centre, the reverse side of the coin is that they were thus given the opportunity to gain considerable influence over the Omugabe. Various early travellers have in fact referred to them as the 'power behind the throne'.[52] Moreover, despite their involvement at the political centre, it appears that the Bakungu retained considerable freedom of action in their own areas. Willis, for instance, who was in Ankole when the British assumed their overrule, and whose refreshingly naive journal affords many useful insights into political relationships during his time, commented in 1901: 'Hitherto each chief had done what he liked...' (and added: 'Now there will be a settled responsible government'.)[53] But while the Bakungu were thus relatively autonomous vis-à-vis the Omugabe, within their own territorial jurisdictions they were themselves restricted in their powers. Roscoe stated it quite strongly: 'The authority of a Mukungu in his own district was limited, for he had no control over the movements of the subordinate chiefs and other people who might take up their residence or pasture their cows there ... There was no animosity between the Mukungu and the subordinate chiefs in his own district, but the latter were quite independent and only acknowledged him as their superior when some dispute arose among them and required authoritative settlement.'[54] It suggests that political power not only was dispersed spatially ('decentralised'), but also did not reach down very deeply.

In these conditions, there was not much the Omugabe could do to enhance his influence, except through his personal leadership qualities. A large number of the senior chiefs were Bahinda, and while they had pledged their loyalty to the Omugabe, the latter was in no small respect dependent upon their continued support. His obligation to cater for their interests was perhaps even stronger since in Nkore there had not developed, as in Bunyoro and Toro, special functions of heads of the royal clan which were distinct from the office of the monarch.[55] This may indicate a lesser amount of political role differentiation in the Nkore situation and suggest that in times of crises, the office of the Omugabe might be more vulnerable to demands by the royal clan than was the case in Bunyoro or Toro.

Moreover, although formally all senior chiefs were appointed by the Omugabe, these appointments in fact tended to confirm, and in a sense disguise, hereditary succession to office. Roscoe wrote that 'When one of these (Bakungu) chiefs died, the king appointed his successor who was generally, though not necessarily, his heir.'[56] Also, the Omugabe may have been able to demote one of them,[57] but then most probably not without the backing of the other Bakungu. There was always the possibility of a chief withdrawing his allegiance, which had to be countered by concessions or punitive measure – depending upon the amount of countervailing strength available. Some Bahinda were in fact potential rivals to the Omugabe. Succession to the kingship was commonly determined in a contest between warring factions of princes, in which victory fell to the one who succeeded in taking possession of Bagyendanwa, the royal drum. 'The choice, therefore', commented a senior prince, 'was spears. Spears are in fact the nation, they indicate where the will of the nation lies.'[58] It was possible, however, that even if one contender had come out victorious and had been installed as Omugabe, rival factions would continue their opposition and consider him as *Ekyebumbe*, a usurper. Full legitimacy was therefore not bestowed upon an Omugabe until all fighting had subsided.[59]

The potential challenge which came from the Bahinda was also exemplified by the rule that the Omugabe's chief adviser, the Enganzi, could not be a member of the royal clan, since a Muhinda might conceivably use his position to seize power. The office of Enganzi was filled either by a Muhima of a non-royal Nkore clan, by a member of a royal clan of a neighbouring kingdom, or even by a Mwiru.[60] These various arrangements are tokens of real or potential limitation to the exercise of power by the Omugabe. If therefore, as Stenning has suggested, 'In Nkore there seems to have been little conflict between the hereditary principle and that of appointment,'[61] then this was appearance rather than actual fact, achieved through a delicate balance of forces in which tension between these principles was contained. Basically, the traditional political structure of Nkore was highly fragile, and its kingship served to provide it with a sense of unity.

Some aspects of the jurisdiction attributed in theory to the Omugabe accordingly present a different picture in practice. For instance, while theoretically the Omugabe was the owner of all land, in actual fact this title had little or no bearing on the way land was allocated. Aside from inheritance, in principle people could occupy a vacant plot unless someone else had an earlier claim on it. In cases of dispute, the issue would be settled by the chiefs. Again, if people desired to move into an area which had not been their traditional habitat, the chief would commonly allocate a stretch of land to them.[62] All these tenure arrangements were naturally of importance to the Bairu cultivators. In respect of the Bairu, it is clear that a man who cultivated a piece of land had certain rights in it, his clan members or neighbours had other rights, the local chief had a further say, while the Omugabe was seen as the notional 'owner' of all land. For the Bahima, again, land was historically of little concern. Not only was it relatively plentiful, but since Bahima were constantly moving with their herds of cattle, there was also little reason for them to submit claims on any particular piece of land.[63]

The Omugabe's 'ownership' of land, therefore, rather than connoting any strictly defined property relationships in a Western legal sense, was primarily a symbol of ultimate control by which legitimate authority over the society was claimed for the Nkore kingship.

Similarly, the Omugabe's theoretical ownership of cattle contrasted in significant respects with reality. In theory, it will be re-called, all cattle belonged to the Omugabe and he 'gave' them to Bahima in reward for their loyalty, particularly in times of war. In practice, however, the relationship appears rather to have been the reverse. Bahima enjoyed virtually unrestricted use of the cattle under their control and paid tribute to the Omugabe through the gift of cows, in return for which they could expect protection from the political centre.[64] The prevalence of this arrangement can be gathered, among other things, from the fact that the Omugabe had his 'own' herds, which were taken for grazing by his herdsmen in various parts of the country. For such cases, the term 'clientship' would seem the proper description and here the 'giving' did indeed initiate with the Omugabe.[65]

However, as this by no means applied to all cattle, and as other senior chiefs similarly entered into such clientship contracts, this contradicts the view that ownership of all cattle in any concrete sense rested with the Omugabe. His theoretical claim to all cattle should be seen rather as a symbolic device to assert the political unity of the Bahima of Nkore, which had little to do with actual control and usufruct arrangements.

Again, the pervasive political role attributed to the Omugabe contrasts markedly with his actual function. As noted, the theoretical claims to absolute rulership need serious qualification in the light of the role of Bakungu and other officials in decision making. Moreover, it appears that the office of the Omugabe was in large part a judicial one. Most of the meetings of the Omugabe's court, the assembly of chiefs, were concerned with settlement of disputes between Bahima litigants, ranging from cases of theft and murder to various other infringements of rights and privileges.[66] Willis attended this council in 1902, and it seems reasonable to assume that his description is in essence applicable to the preceding precolonial period :

> The Native Council ... is delightfully informal ... The King and Katikiro sit at one end...and all the chiefs are arranged in more or less order of precedence, down two sides, the poorer people thronging near the door. There is no attempt at any formal opening: no one stands up to address the rest, for all are speaking at once. In the midst of business anyone who likes strolls up, bows down, and salutes the King in a loud voice.
>
> Most of the business consists of hearing (!) cases, for the Council is a rough and ready Court of Justice. Witnesses are of course entirely unnecessary. Two scantily clad men, unannounced, come in: each begins accusing the other violently to the King...
>
> ...(The) claimant, finding the King otherwise engaged, looks anxiously around for someone who appears to be listening and shouts at him. By this time the discussion has become general, and everyone is talking at the top of his voice : no one hears anyone, for everyone is shouting. The marvel is that out of the hubbub, a verdict emerges, given quite decisively and without hesitation.[67]

The nature of the cases dealt with by this court was no doubt more varied than those before any ordinary modern court, covering matters of administration and politics as well as more narrowly defined 'legal' issues. Of key importance was also the fact that in all the cases brought before them, '(The) function of the Mugabe and his chiefs lay more in giving judgements than in meting out punishments'.[67] Moreover, 'there was no police organization to guard life and property'. Instead, as in the case of murder, 'the Mugabe would grant the right of blood revenge, which, however, had to be carried out by the members of the injured extended family'.

The structural implications of this are of no small significance. *Prima facie*, the arrangements would appear to re-emphasise the limitations to the Omugabe's powers. However, the importance of his role should not necessarily be judged primarily by his executive powers. As with kingship in ancient times, the essence of Nkore kingship was law-giving. This was not carried out by the promulgation of sets of abstract regulations to which behaviour would henceforth need to conform. That would only have made sense if there had been a body of specialised agents, an administration and a 'police organisation', to whom the task of applying such rules could be delegated. In Nkore, where the Bakungu were involved in the law-making process, such a body was lacking. Law-giving in traditional Nkore appears rather to have been a matter of articulating the considered opinion of the leading members of the society on questions of social behaviour for which the solution was either not quite obvious or involved such drastic action to settle that a higher sanction was necessary. In either case, there was recourse to what was known as the law of the land and it was this to which the Omugabe finally gave expression. Kinyankore law was a living code, and its function was probably even more important than that of law in a society with more specialised organs of government. For it would appear that nothing less than the cohesiveness of the political community depended largely on the meaningfulness of the judgements passed on the relationships between its members.

The limits of power of Nkore kingship

Evidently, as we have seen, while in theory the Omugabe was all-powerful, in reality his powers were quite limited. In theory, he was the supreme decision-maker, but in practice the system depended heavily on reaching agreement among the political elite. Again, in theory the Omugabe could rely on coercion to have his will followed, but in practice he depended largely on voluntary compliance with the judgements he pronounced.

Several possible explanations can be advanced to account for these apparent contradictions. The easiest of course, but also the least valid, would be to regard them as mutually exclusive interpretations, of which one must be necessarily wrong. The Omugabe was neither the mighty *Rubambansi* nor the more humble *primus inter pares*; from Nkore tradition we learn that somehow he was both. Instead, it is more meaningful to recognise both notions as valid and try to account for their co-existence and interrelationships. Several approaches suggest themselves if the two notions of the Nkore monarchy are treated as different perceptions or different aspects of kingship. Either can be further distinguished into conflicting or complementary notions.

Let us first consider these images as different perceptions. The idea that the Omugabe was omnipotent versus the idea that he was no more than a mediator might then reflect the contrasting ways in which the power of kingship was perceived by different social strata or territorial groups. There can be little doubt that the perceptions people held of the office of the Omugabe were different at various levels of the social structure. Historically, Bairu are more likely than the Bahima to have regarded the Omugabe as a despotic and powerful, though distant, ruler. Again, in some newly subjugated areas, the power face of the kingship may have appeared more in evidence than in the core of the kingdom, since people commonly attribute domination to its leadership.[69] Such different perceptions, then, would conflict with and contradict each other if one takes the narrow view that there can be only one 'true' manifestation of the institution one analyses, and that, accordingly, kingship here would only allow a singular definition. But they are complementary and reconcilable if one starts from the view point that they can illuminate equally valid perceptions, from different vantage points in the system, of the institution.

These points thus indicate how, from 'the outside' as it were, the same institution can be differently perceived. While these differences may offer a partial explanation for the *Rubambansi* versus *primus inter pares* 'paradox', for additional insights we will need to look 'inside' the structure.[70] This we can do by looking at the two images of the Omugabe as aspects of the same institutional set-up. As aspects of the same structure, the notions of the Omugabe as the powerful *Rubambansi* or as the more common *primus inter pares* can also be seen as conflicting or complementary. They conflict if one holds that the system does not function on the basis of a single governing principle, but that there is an underlying ambivalence between two contradictory criteria which have roughly equal relevance. One particular form of such ambivalence, a tension between semi-feudal and bureaucratic elements, has been suggested by Audrey Richards as applicable to the interlacustrine area as a whole. Richards argued that :

> (in) all these tribes, kings and kinglets (sic) seem to have felt the need to bolster up their powers as against the hereditary elements, not only the princes, but also the different clan authorities who formerly ruled in semi-independent fashion over their people. The followers or clients whom the rulers appointed as administrative heads over districts or groups of villages, or to executive posts at the capital were the men on whom they began to rely for support. It is in fact the balance of power between these two elements, the hereditary and the appointed, which makes for the variation in the pattern of these conquest states.[71]

If this dichotomy is applied to Nkore, the two existing notions of the political structure would be explicable by reference to structural tension between, on the one hand, an Omugabe who seeks to impose his command on the system and, on the other, a number of more or less autonomous hereditary power clusters which resist this. The *Rubambansi* idea would stress the powers of the state, while the *primus inter pares* notion emphasises the influence of hereditary elements.

A somewhat different way of looking at the two notions as conflicting aspects of the power structure would be to consider them not as in the above as real opposite forces pulling in other directions. But to identify the *Rubambansi* aspect as the ideal one and the *primus inter pares* aspect as the *actual*. This would conform to a kind of distinction made by anthropologists since Malinowski, especially with Leach's formulation.[72] In this view, inconsistency and conflict between the two notions would be recognised, conflict occurring between what is ideally prescribed, on the one hand, and the way matters are actually worked out, on the other. Specifically, against the background of this distinction, the Omugabe would appear a politically rather frustrated man continuously making appeals to the Bakungu to recognise the supreme powers he was granted and to comply rather than interfere with his commands.

For complementary aspects, the model at hand is that of Dahrendorf in which the two pictures of the Nkore political structure correspond roughly to the two postulated faces of social structure: coercion and integration.[73] It is true that no political system is solely maintained on the basis of power and domination. And no system exists only by virtue of freely given support. While in some systems the coercive aspect is more salient than in others, all essentially feature both aspects. In this perspective, the contradiction would result from ideological or scholarly preferences emphasising one or other of the two aspects of social structure which are inherent in any organisation. Projected onto Nkore, the *Rubambansi* notion would represent the coercive aspect, and the *primus inter pares* notion the integrative aspect of the political structure.

Thus, we have a variety of models available with which to interpret the role and apparent paradox of Nkore kingship, each of which might teach us something useful. Each model focuses on a particular facet of the reality situation, which is inevitably complex and inconsistent.[74] Real societies are not blueprints, but over time a variety of designs may have gone into their building. Hence, different, at times even contradictory, images of real systems are obtained, depending on the focus and indicators applied in the analysis. But while there is no gainsaying the validity per se of any model, some are clearly better equipped to elucidate the key characteristics of a system than others. For the Nkore case, the models we have seen are not adequate to explain its special features. For instance, to interpret the traditional Nkore system on the basis of a hereditary-appointive dichotomy is not 'wrong', but is directed at only one and not necessarily the most relevant aspect of the system. Similar limitations are inherent in the other approaches. The distinction between ideal and actual powers of kingship, seen as conflicting aspects, is quite legitimate, but there is no evidence that tension along these lines lay at the heart of the political process in Nkore. Again, while basically appropriate, the coercion-integration hypothesis is too general to illuminate the distinctive features of the Nkore political system.

Considering the characteristics of Nkore kingship, we might more fruitfully turn to another model which combines some of the above elements in a new fashion and focuses on a structural relationship not touched upon in the other models. This model also involves postulating the two images of the Nkore system as complementary aspects. However, these aspects should not be regarded as two faces of one coin, as in the Dahrendorf model, but as each other's functional complements. While this is related to the idea of ambivalence of principles on which the political structure may be based (as in the hereditary-appointive or idea-actual distinctions), one should not *a priori* assume conflict between the criteria. The assumption is rather that the Nkore system was able to function the way it did, and perhaps to function at all, because of the way in which the two notions of power complemented one another.

We have seen that the Nkore system was highly vulnerable to fragmentation due to the claims of Bahinda and other Bahima. The absence of a cadre of officials solely loyal to the political centre meant that the integration of the system could only be maintained by invoking higher values to sanction decisions which had been arrived at through debate and majority opinion. At the elite level, there was widespread participation in the decision-making process, which had to cope with conflicting interests and fairly autonomous political strongholds in the system. Inevitably, therefore, two closely related problems presented themselves when decisions were being made.

Firstly, if they were to be believable, it was essential that decisions should have an aura of higher sanctity than would be normally associated with the opinion of a body of individuals, even if these were leading members of society. If justice and law were to be more than a bargain, they had to be characterised by universalistic and transcendental qualities which should be able to command acceptance. If the Omugabe had been actually an absolute ruler, presumably he would have been considered as embodying these qualities. But as he was not, the attribution of omnipotence and ultimate benevolence which was bestowed upon him still served to sanction the *communis opinio* which it was his prerogative to articulate.

Secondly, once a decision had been taken, the problem was to secure adherence to the judgement passed. In the absence of the machinery for implementation, compliance basically rested with mechanisms of social control. Here, too, the exalted notion of the Omugabe as a political giant wielding unlimited powers came in, not to conflict with, but to complement the characteristics of the political structure. Decisions carried weight because they were ordained in the name of high authority, even if this authority was highly symbolic and only partly involved direct control over subordinates.

The coherence of the political community depended critically on maintaining this myth, which was its main antidote to centrifugal tendencies. The myth's personification, the Omugabe, who transposed elite deliberation into state law, constituted the major formal institution of the Bahima state. Indeed, he had sounder grounds than Louis XIV on which to claim *L'etat c'est moi*. Hence, it was towards and through the validation of this myth that an effective synthesis between two seemingly contradictory notions of kingship was obtained. The relationship between the distribution of political power and values about authority thus formed a very central axis in the traditional Nkore system.

Notes

1 The main text for this essay was drafted before publication of S. R. Karugire, *A History of the Kingdom of Nkore in Western Uganda to 1896*, Oxford, 1971, which may be usefully consulted on various aspects of Nkore kingship.
2 The main societies adjacent to Nkore are named here as they were known just prior to the colonial intervention.
3 G.N. Uzoigwe, 'Pre-colonial Markets in Bunyoro-Kitara', *Comparative Studies in Society and History*, XXIV, 4, 1972: 441-45.
4 J. B. Webster, (ed.), *Uganda Before 1900*, vol. I, Nairobi, 1973. Introduction. Cf. also John Beattie, *Bunyoro, An African Kingdom*, New York, 1960:16-17.
5 Cf. Brian K. Taylor, The *Western Lacustrine Bantu*, London, 1962; Richards, op. cit.
6 Uganda Protectorate, Report on the Runyankore-Rukiga Orthographic Conference, Government Printer, 1956.
7 Mungonya, *op.cit.*; Wrigley, *op.cit.* Some mythological parallels can be found even further afield, cf. Luc de Heusch, *Le Roi Ivre ou l'origine de l'Etat*, Paris, 1972.
8 H. F. Morris, *A History of Ankole*, Kampala, 1962: 6. Even in Ankole there are further variations to the tale. A distinctly Bairu version is related in P. I. Gorju, *Entre le Victoria, l'Albert et l'Edouard*, Refines, 1920: 279-81.
9 For an interesting speculation about the relationship between ecology, crops and the development of political organisation in parts of the interlacustrine area, see Conrad P. Kottak, 'Ecological variables in the Origin and Evolution of African States: the Buganda Example', *Comparative Studies in Society and History*, XIV, 3, 1972.
10 Cf. D. J. Stenning. 'Salvation in Ankole', in M. Fortes and G. Dieterlen. (eds), *African Systems of Thought*, London. 1965: 268.
11 Uzoigwe. *op. cit.* 444:47.
12 M. T. Mushanga, 'The Clan System among the Banyankore', *Uganda Journal*, XXXIV. 1. 1970: 29-33.
13 In Ankole, for instance, this appears to have been true for the Abasingo clan. Cf. Karugire, *op.cit.*, 51.

14 The primary example of a three-tiered pattern of ethnic stratification was Rwanda, where Batutsi, Bahutu and the tiny minority of Batwa were ranked in an order of decreasing prominence. See Jacques I. Maquet, *The Premise of Inequality*, London, 1961.
15 Maquet, *op. cit.*; Rene Lemarchand, *Rwanda and Burundi* London, 1970.
16 The break-away of Toro from Bunyoro-Kitara and Toro's own vulnerability to centripetal forces-especially in Busongora, Kitagwenda and Kibage-illustrated this tendency.
17 All major historical sources thus far have been concentrated on Nkore: John Roscoe, *The Banyankore*, Cambridge, 1923; K. Oberg, 'The Kingdom of Ankole in Uganda', 'in M. Fortes and E. E. Evans-Pritchard (eds) *African Political Systems*, London, 1940; A. G.Katate and L. Kamugungunu, *Abagabe b' Ankole*, Ekitabo I and II, Kampala, 1955; Morris, *op. cit.*, Karugire, *op. cit.*
18 cf. D. J. Stenning, 'The 'Nyankole', in Audrey I. Richards, ed., *East African Chiefs: 154*.
19 For an interpretation of historical change in the Nkore kingdom, see Karugire, *op.cit.*
20 D. I. Stenning, 'The Nyankole': 153.
21 In the present century Bairu have acquired increasing numbers of cattle and as early as 1938 owned almost as many head as the Bahima did. See W. L. S. Mackintosh, *Some notes on the Bahima and the Cattle Industry in Ankole*, Mbarara, 1938. Today, the total Bairu ownership of cattle almost certainly surpasses that of the Bahima.
22 The 1969 census figures, indicating a total population of 861,145, have not distinguished between Ankole's ethnic groups *(1971 Statistical Abstract* :10.) But it may be estimated that the Bairu account for about 90 per cent of the population, the remainder being made up by Bahima and relatively recent immigrant groups, especially Bakiga from the neighbouring Kigezi district.
23 Still, Johnston in 1902 cites information suggesting that 'the Hima population and their stock of cattle at the present day (are) not more than a 'third of what they were fourteen years ago'. Sir Harry Johnston, *The Uganda Protectorate*, Vol. II, London. 1902: 626.
24 J. H. Speke, *Journal of the Discovery of the Source of the Nile*, London 1863: 246.
25 Inevitably, the discussion has led to various speculations as to the presumed area of origin of the Bahima. Whereas it has usually been assumed that Bairu were indigenous to the area, an astounding perplexity of origins has been attributed to the Bahima, most often Ethiopia and Somalia, but also ancient Egypt as well as ancient Israel. See J. F. Cunningham, *Uganda and its People* (London, 1905) : x-xi; Sir Harry Johnston, *The Uganda Protectorate*, Vol 1, (London 1902) : 210; Robert P. Ashe, *Two Kings of Uganda* (London 1889):337-38. Sir Albert R. Cook summarises a good deal of the early opinion on the Bahima by stating that: 'everyone has remarked their extra-ordinary likeness to the old Egyptian mummies', and Alfred R. Tucker describes the typical Muhima as 'a man the very image, you would say, of Ramses II'. Sir Albert R. Cook, *Uganda Memories (1897-1940),* (Kampala, 1945): 118; Alfred R. Tucker, *Eighteen Years in Uganda and East Africa*, (London, 1911):272. Recently, the debate has shifted to biochemical arguments, although as it seems, not yet with conclusive proof. See Merrick Posnansky, 'Kingship, Archaeology and Historical Myth', *Uganda Journal*, 30,1,1966: 6-7 for a dismissal of theories of extraneous origin because of lack of archeological evidence, and the alternative hypothesis that Bairu and Bahima may have originated from the same stock, but developed different physiques as a result of contrasting diets; and G. C. Cook, 'Tribal Incidence of Lactose Deficiency, in Uganda', *The Lancet*, April 2, 1966: 725-30, for an analysis of different lactose resistance which appears to reaffirm the suggestion of 'original' differences between Bairu and Bahima.
26 Kottak, *op.cit.*, 351-53. He pointedly adds: 'Perhaps scholars have assumed, having witnessed so many examples of European conquest and colonialism in non-European areas, that this is the only, or the 'principal way, in which a societal form can be changed.'

27 F. Lukyn-Williams, 'The Inauguration of the Omugabe of Ankole to Office', *Uganda Journal*, IV, 4, 1937:309. See also Karugire, *op.cit.*, p.97.
28 As is implied in the Nkore mythical charter, cited above.
29 The term 'Bahima state' was used by Oberg (*Op.cit*, 128). While Oberg's account of the traditional system needs qualification, there are good grounds to borrow the notion of a 'Bahima state' as a shorthand designation of the Nkore political structure. See also below.
30 In the light of speculations about ethnic 'origins', the common clan system of Bairu and Bahima is intriguing. Assuming different origins, in Ankole today two explanations are offered. One, mostly advanced by Bahima, holds that the incoming Bahima 'reorganised' the Bairu into 'followings' that still account for the present common clan membership. Another, more distinctly Bairu interpretation, suggests that the 'invading' Bahima found an existing (Bairu) clan organisation, which they found suitable as a means of control and for purposes of acculturation. The latter view can be related to Lukyn-Williams' observation that 'there is little doubt that we have in Ankole ... an example, by no means unknown throughout the world, of a conquering race adopting the language and customs of the conquered, while at the same time keeping themselves separate.' Lukyn-Wiliams, *op.cit.*, 33-34. In the absence of conclusive evidence on the origins of Bairu and Bahima both explanations are highly speculative and perhaps are primarily political rationalisations.
31 Mushanga, *op.cit.*
32 Today the exceptions cited are rather of educated Bairu men marrying educated Bahima girls.
33 Analyses of Nkore have often insufficiently recognized this basic point. As a result, images of more pervasive ethnic domination than obtained in reality tended to be conveyed; e.g. Oberg *op. cit.*, p. 134; Stenning, 'The Nyankole', p. 169. See further my paper 'Images and Reality of Stratification in Pre-colonial Nkore', *Canadian Journal of African Studies*, VII, 3, 1973.
34 Cf. Oberg, *op.cit*, 129-130; Mackintosh, *op.cit.*, 20; Stenning, 'The Nyankole' : 152.
35 Oberg, *op. cit.*, 128-36; see also Jacques Maquet, 'Institutionalisation Feodale des relations de dependence dans quatre cultures interlacustrines'. *Colloque du Groupe de Recherches en Anthropologie et Sociologie Politique*, Paris, 1968, (mimeo).
36 Cf. Oberg, *op.cit.*, 131; Stenning, *op.cit.*, 153.
37 Again it must be stressed that it is beyond the scope of this study to differentiate between the Nkore political organisation of one period and the next. Thus, it may well be that the Omugabe was gradually moving to a more powerful position, as happened in Buganda (see Martin Southwold, *Bureaucracy and Chiefship in Buganda*, East African Studies, No. 14, Kampala, 1961), or else that his position was growing weaker, but our information does not enable us to validate either hypothesis. See, however, Karugire, *op.cit.*
38 See the insightful discussion of Peter C. Lloyd, 'The Political Structure of Mrioan Kingdoms: An Exploratory Model', in M. Banton, ed., *Political Systems and the Distribution of Power*, London, 1965 : 63-112.
39 An exception is Karugire (op.cit.), who on the subject of Nkore kingship offers a useful and balanced analysis.
40 Roscoe, *op.cit*, 12.
41 *Ibid.*, 36.
42 Mackintosh, *op.cit.*, 13.
43 Oberg, *op.cit.*, 136-37.
44 Ntare School History Society, 'The Governmental institutions in Ankole before the British Rule', (mimeo Mbarara, n.d. 1965)
45 I.Vansina, 'A Comparison of African Kingdoms', *Africa*, XXXll, 4, 1962: 332.
46 The implied analogy is to a characteristic Bahima skill, namely the stretching of a cow's hide.

47 H. F. Morris (ed.), *The Heroic Recitations of the Bahima of Ankole*, Oxford, 1964: Cf. also Oberg, *op.cit.,* p. 136, According to some Banyankore, the present spelling of the word 'Omugabe' carries Luganda influences. Although the term does have historical roots, in past times the king was more commonly addressed as 'Omukama'. In the earlier colonial period, the British referred to him as 'Kabaka', as they then did to all traditional rulers in Uganda. The term Omugabe appears to have become more prevalent since roughly the 1930s.
48 Lukyn-Williams, *op.cit.*, 312.
49 Roscoe, *op.cit.*, p. 51. Cf. also Robert H. Lowie, *Social Organization*, London, 1950: 344-345.
50 Cf. Karugire, *op.cit.*, 105-06. For an analysis of a comparable situation, consult the discussion of .the symbolic and political roles of Bunyoro kingship in Beattie, *op. cit.*, 25-41.
51 Cf. Oberg, *op.cit.*, 134.
52 E.g. Tucker, *op. cit.*, 272.
53 *Willis Journal* 11, unpublished (a copy of this journal is deposited in the Library of Makerere University, Kampala) : 228.
54 Roscoe, *op.cit.*, 15-16.
55 Beattie, *op.cit.*, 31; Taylor, *op.cit*, 35, 62.
56 Roscoe, *op.cit.*, 14
57 Stenning, 'The Nyankole' : 157.
58 Transcript of a discussion with the Omugabe and senior princes of Ankole, 27 September 1966, recorded by Mr Gersham Nshemereirwe. The point was made by Mr Samwiri Rwabushongo.
59 *Ibid.*
60 The selection of a Muhima of a non-royal clan appears to have been the general rule. Nuwa Mbaguta, who was Enganzi at the establishment of British rule, was a member of the royal clan of another kingdom, Mpororo. Muhigi, the Enganzi of Ntare V, was a Mwiru, although of a clan which was gradually moving to higher social status, the Basingo.
61 Stenning, 'The Nyankole' : 157.
62 Roscoe, *op.cit.*, 95.
63 Mackintosh, *op.cit.*, 12.
64 Oberg, *op.cit.*, 129; cf. Maquet, 'Institutionalisation feodale', 2.
65 Roscoe, *op.cit.*, 15-16.
66 Stenning, 'The Nyankole', 152.
67 Willis Journal, II, 290-91.
68 Oberg, *op.cit.*, 133-34.
69 Cf. Rene Lemarchand, 'Power and Stratification in Rwanda: A Reconsideration', *Cahiers d'Etudes*, VI, 4, 1966, 597-98.
70 At the risk of tediousness, we should also recognise that different perceptions, giving rise to different interpretations, may well originate with the people who record the evidence. Thus, different perspectives, of analysts, can be related, or in fact lead, to different aspects of an institution being emphasised in attempts to explain its structuring or operation.
71 Richards, *East African Chiefs: 138.* See also L. Pallets, 'The Predicament of the Modern African Chief', *American Anthropologist,* LVII, 2, 1955 *passim.*
72 E.R. Leach, *Political Systems of Highland Burma* London, 1954: 8-15.
73 Raf Dahrendolf, *Class and Class Conflict in Industrial Society* London, 1959: 157-73.
74 Leach, *op.cit.*, 8.

3
Incorporation and Expansion

In the preceding chapter we have outlined some of the distinctive features of Nkore kingship and the setting in which it functioned. We also considered some alternative analytical models in an attempt to understand the Nkore power structure, particularly its apparent contradiction of images of extensive monarchical power and the Omugabe's role as *primus inter pares*. We can now proceed to analyse the transformations to which the institution was subject during colonial times. First, however, a word on perceptions is necessary.

In the analysis of African social change colonial intervention has frequently been taken as a major baseline. The pre-colonial situation is described first and is then contrasted with subsequent developments during colonialism. But all too often the effort has been oriented towards one or the other of two purposes and perspectives. In the one, the focus is on the distinctive characteristics and cultural attributes of one particular society, which are supposedly rooted in 'tradition' and which the analyst, who sets out to identify their effects and persistence, traces through the colonial period, and beyond, to document the special way in which change has been mediated and 'accommodated' in that particular case. One thus derives 'continuity of culture', a theme which has long been pervasive in much of the anthropological and historical literature on single African societies – both small-scale systems and historic states –incorporated into colonial frameworks.

In the other perspective, much of the detail is left aside and the focus itself is different. Again colonial intervention is handled as a major historical watershed, but as one from which point onwards African societies are seen as being increasingly shaped after the image of the colonising Western powers, – whether as 'modernising' entities or as the exploited reservoirs of human and material resources. Thus, instead of an emphasis on what is distinctive or culturally specific, the stress is here on the general forces and consequences of colonialism and imperialism. 'Tradition' becomes a residual category, and the specific sociopolitical features of any particular African society may figure relatively little in the analysis of change, or else be dealt with separately from the 'modern' influences so that a certain inexplicitness remains as to how exactly colonial processes impinged upon and transformed a particular social framework.

These differences are matters of emphasis related in part to different disciplinary traditions, in part to other kinds of preferences. But as emphases go, they can illuminate one thing and eclipse another. The present analysis also tries to come to grips with processes of change provoked by colonialism and is similarly based on a before and after procedure. But the interest that underlies it is to grasp the effects of colonial arrangements on one society, Ankole, and particularly its institution of kingship. We will therefore be concerned with change rather than continuity and without losing sight of the 'general' effects of European colonisation, we will try to examine their specific repercussions within the Ankole sociopolitical context.

Thus, among the salient characteristics of the historic Nkore system, we have noted there was a basic social and economic separateness of Bairu and Bahima, a certain power advantage held by the Bahima vis-à-vis the Bairu, and an institution of kingship of which the incumbent acted largely as a *primus inter pares* among the political elite. Colonial rule profoundly affected these arrangements. Its different and externally determined modes of political control, the introduction of market mechanisms, the re-direction of production processes and other impacts it had on social relationships, were among the major departures which, in Ankole as elsewhere, began to generate a new species of society dependent and run largely on a basis of peasant production plus law and order. These effects, to be sure, were fundamentally 'general', as was also the corollary emergence of class phenomena within the new bureaucratic salariat. But in a society that had its own, quite specific pattern of ethnic cum occupational groupings and a rather distinctive institutional structure, these general effects could hardly but manifest themselves in a similarly specific way. They produced new cleavages and frictions that also need to be understood against the dynamics and forces which distinguished this context.

Our argument thus will run roughly as follows. Notwithstanding a semblance of 'Indirect Rule' and institutional continuity, colonisation in the case of Ankole (as elsewhere in Uganda) meant the establishment of a colonial administrative state. This administrative state implied the creation of a new chiefly elite, whose sociopolitical status was derived from, and defined by, the colonial framework. By virtue of the 'franchise'[1] and benefits granted to this elite, and (thus) also in the absence of alternative powerful ranking criteria, this group's strategic position turned them into a privileged elite and a local ruling class.

These arrangements, however, resulted in two peculiar constellations in Ankole. One, either a matter of historical misconception or of deliberate strategy, was that Bahima were recruited in a disproportionately large number into the senior ranks of this chiefly class. This practice in any event entailed a self-implementing hypothesis: that historical Nkore had been based on an ethnic hierarchy, with Bahima on top and Bairu at the bottom. In turn it also entailed an inbuilt ethnic friction, as Bairu in due course began to question and challenge the basis of allocation of these political rewards. The other peculiarity pertained to the role of kingship. Nominally, this posed as a mythical umbrella underneath which colonial transformations took shape, but in reality it was used as an instrument of colonial rule. But partly due to the colonial lack of appreciation of the historical role of kingship, the institution could not prove itself very effective at this new task, while moreover its lack of 'fit' inevitably became even more problematic due to the Bairu-Bahima division.

But while colonialism set in motion various far-reaching processes in Ankole, not all of their consequences were evident at once. For some transformations to become more visible a certain time period would have to lapse. Their basic starting points can nonetheless be identified, at the juncture where new politico-administrative structures were imposed upon the society.

Accordingly, for purposes of our discussion, rather than delve much into the events of the late 1890s, when colonial contact was first established, it will be more fruitful for us to concentrate on the basic patterns that resulted from it. It is not necessary to have any exact moment in time as such a point of departure, though if one were to give a date at all, 1901 would seem the most appropriate. It was then that the Ankole Agreement was concluded between the British and the local notables, consolidating much that had been arranged during initial contacts. At the same time, the agreement heralded several major transformations, namely: (a) the expansion of scale of Ankole, (b) the incorporation of Ankole into Uganda, (c) the reduction of Bahinda influence, (d) the restructuring of the position of the Omugabe and (e) the transformation of the ethnic division. Each of these developments, as we shall see, had drastic effects on the role of the kingship.

Ankole and the Uganda context

At the turn of the century, the single most important measure pertaining to Ankole was obviously its incorporation into the Uganda framework. The British had had their influence established in adjacent Buganda for some time when, after the 1884 Berlin conference, they extended their interest further west and north. In the case of Toro (1900) and Ankole (1901), this expansion was formalised through 'treaties' with the royalty and chiefs of the two kingdoms. Bunyoro, which had resisted British intrusion – realised nonetheless with the close support of its rival, Buganda – was given the status of 'agreement state' similar to that of Ankole and Toro only in 1933. None of these three agreements provided for delegation of similar powers and prerogatives as had been given to Buganda (1894). They were largely nominal recognitions, though nonetheless with some discernible effects on local status categorisations.

That Ankole was brought into the wider orbit of Uganda was evidently of far-reaching consequence, since from that moment the perpetuation of its political system rested no longer on any intrinsic strength but depended basically on considerations of political expediency which were extraneous to Ankole. Initially, there was the familiar stratagem of employing traditional structures of authority, if only in rudimentary fashion, as a convenient way of gaining colonial control. Before long, however, this rationale lost much of its strength as the colonial administrative network itself gained in effectiveness. Ankole soon became fully immersed in this network, although a sense of distinctiveness, partly based on the retention of the kingship, was maintained throughout. This, as we shall see, was to be made use of even as late as the post-independence period in order to counteract the dominant weight and image of Buganda.

Even if exercised with the utmost benevolence, in the early self-confident period colonial rule was strongly authoritarian. It established a bureaucratic state in which actions originated as a result of orders sent down by more highly placed officials to their subordinates and in which elaborate reporting at all levels placed further controls upon the execution of policies. Its prevailing tone was one of a briskness between sportsmanship and military style.[2] Its values were rational and concrete and centred upon law and order. Its lines of command comprised colonial officers as well as African chiefs, and while the distinction between these ranks was strenuously maintained, both had to observe comparable criteria of hierachy and administrative competence.

These qualities applied in Ankole as much as they did elsewhere. The dispersed power structure of the traditional Nkore system was replaced by a hierarchical framework, while concrete and pragmatic values were substituted for the metaphysical authority notions of the traditional system. The link between traditional values and the traditional authority structure became altogether lost in the process and the effect of this was to eliminate the role of kingship 'old style'. A semblance of continuity was kept up, however, for the Omugabe was retained and old values were still being referred to. But the essence of the changes was to turn the Omugabe into an instrument of bureaucratic hierarchy, and to relegate traditional values to the level of folklore.

The colonial apparatus into which the kingdom was fitted developed from rather humble beginnings. In Ankole, unlike some other cases, establishing the British presence did not involve prolonged violence. Somewhat euphemistically, a former governor of Uganda described the process in this fashion:

> a British officer could arrive at some remote place, as I have myself done, accompanied only by a couple of native policemen and perhaps a clerk or two, and carrying with him a union jack, uniforms and rifles for the score of local policemen to be enlisted, and the requisite stationary [sic] and books, and in a few weeks have some sort of government functioning ... (If) there was

acquiescence, as was usual, there was ready to hand a piece of machinery which might be primitive, but was in working order.³

From that point, at any rate, there tended to be a steady expansion, and consolidation, of the administrative framework, and almost invariably the piece of machinery showed itself capable of coping with a rapidly increasing number of tasks. Boundaries were drawn and redrawn between administrative divisions and sub-divisions; administrative ranks of county, sub-county and village chiefs as well as a host of other positions were created; and, in a never-ending flow of directives, the tasks of all these officials were specified in ever greater detail. The result of it all was that the whole district was converted into a single system of command.

At the pinnacle of this structure stood the district commissioner (in the very early days known as the 'collector') in whom executive authority within the district was vested. To him an elaborate cadre of civil servants, African and European, were made responsible. This meant, in fact, that 'Not only must the District Commissioner supervise the "Chiefs"; his responsibilities extend to the conduct of every minor official down to the village clerk or constable.' The 'Bwana D.C.' on tour of the district became a familiar sight and reputedly he was always expected to outpace the Africans accompanying him as a way of asserting his prestige. To the district commissioner were added assistant district commissioner, police, law and public works officers, and as time went by an increasing number of specialised officials were put in charge of such fields as agriculture, forestry, health, veterinary services, marketing and social welfare. The district commissioner himself was accountable, always through the provincial commissioner, to the governor of Uganda, and final responsibility for the conduct of affairs in the protectorate rested, of course, with the British colonial secretary.

Taken together, the establishment of this whole complex amounted to the creation of an administrative state, which in some sense could be said to have been superimposed upon the traditional framework, but which should more properly be viewed as replacing it. Only much later, in the period after the Second World War, did a policy of delegation of administrative functions introduce important changes in this structure. An expanding number of administrative tasks was then devolve upon African local authorities, themselves in large part new creations. But at its establishment, at least, colonial rule was characterised by strong centralisation rather than decentralisation, a quality which was very much evinced through the measures it introduced.

As a way of facilitating their entry into Ankole, the British had promised, in the Ankole Agreement of 1901, the Omugabe and other senior chiefs the right to nominate their successors.⁴ In addition, they were to enjoy some other amenities, such as a share of the revenue collected, land grants, and various other fringe benefits. By the agreement, the 'Chief' Kahaya was 'recognised by His Majesty's Government as the Kabaka or supreme chief' of Ankole, and it was further stipulated that 'so long as the afore-said Kabaka and chiefs abide by the conditions of this Agreement they shall continue to be recognised by His Majesty's Government as the responsible chiefs of the Ankole district.' However, the document added the stick to the carrot, for it was made explicit that, should they fail to abide by its stipulations, removal from office might follow. It was threatened that 'should the Kabaka of Ankole – Kahaya or his successors – be responsible for the infringement of any part of the terms of this Agreement, it shall be open to His Majesty's Government to annul the said Agreement, and to substitute for it any other methods of administering the Ankole district which may seem suitable.' Clearly, the terms of the Ankole Agreement were British, just as the new order it inaugurated.

The conditions under which this treaty was concluded are not without interest, partly because the only available text of the agreement was written in English. The missionary Willis, who had barely begun learning Runyankore, was invited to attend the ceremony only to find out, to his utter despair, that he was asked to give an off-the-cuff interpretation of the agreement in that language.[6] Local understanding apparently was not considered a crucial element, as long as the Ankole representatives duly placed their X-marks, which they readily did. Eventually, it transpired that the agreement, while repeatedly recognised as a 'valid' document, had no particular force of law, or at least not if Banyankore wanted to base an appeal on it.[7] The agreement laid the basis for the incorporation and maintenance of Ankole as a kingdom within the colonial framework. Regulations governing many kinds of behaviour were put on the books and applied just the same way as elsewhere in Uganda, and notwithstanding the eloquent references made to the Ankole Agreement in subsequent documents and public speeches, in the final analysis its function was hardly more than to provide a convenient cloak for the exercise of power by the British.

Whether or not they were aware of what they had been contracted into, at first the Omugabe and chiefs of Ankole were not unwilling to comply with British directives. Of course, they had no choice. But aside from that, British backing provided a new, and perhaps an even more secure, basis for the enjoyment of prerogatives. Moreover, a semblance of traditional authority was kept up, which tended to conceal the loss of status suffered by the incumbents. To the average villager or herdsman, at any rate, the implications of the take-over were not immediately visible. There followed a period of incubation, during which the old order continued to shape popular allegiances (although for decreasing numbers of people), making it possible for the

Omugabe and chiefs to draw upon residual traditional allegiances. The colonial administration was naturally interested in making use of this goodwill to facilitate their own entry and consolidation of control; hence one major consideration suggesting the retention of traditional authorities. Moreover, it was felt, in Ankole as elsewhere, that to remove traditional chiefs might cause consternation and resistance, and such reactions were definitely to be avoided. On these grounds, the Omugabe and his chiefs were enlisted in the service of His Majesty's government. Nonetheless, we shall see that many senior chiefs were replaced much sooner than was anticipated.

Ankole's expansion in scale

Simultaneous to Ankole's incorporation into Uganda, the kingdom itself experienced considerable expansion, a development which constituted another crucial base line. After the redrawing of the kingdom's boundaries, at the turn of the century, Ankole came to comprise an area which was more than twice the size of the nineteenth-century kingdom of Nkore. This spectacular expansion was a result of conquest as well as of colonial policy. Spheres of influence in the interlacustrine area had always fluctuated, but during the latter half of the nineteenth-century Nkore ascended to a considerably enhanced role in the region. As we have seen, this 'imperialism' of Nkore was directly related to the decline of its northern neighbour, Bunyoro, and ran parallel to the growth in power of Buganda. Igara, Buhweju and Buzimba had been made to recognise Nkore's paramountcy and pay tribute to its ruler.

Then, at the turn of the century, the British assumed control over the entire region and subdued additional areas, including Bunyaruguru as well as almost all principalities of Mpororo. Thus, in addition to the original Nkore kingdom (which it should be kept in mind lay in the present Isingiro, Kashari and Nyabushozi counties), Ankole's expansion was largely based on the annexations to the west of Rwampara and Shema counties and of Igara, Bunyaruguru, Buhweju and Mitoma to the north (the latter at the expense of Bunyoro).[8] Following these operations, the parts added by the British, as well as the areas over which Nkore had begun to claim suzerainty, were all firmly amalgamated with Ankole. Formal expression was given to these annexations in the Ankole Agreement of 1901. Kajara was not added until later. In this agreement the administrative divisions of 'the District of Ankole' were specified as follows:

    (a)   Mitoma
    (b)   Nyabushozi
    (c)   Nshara
    (d)   Isingiro

	(e)	Rwampara
	(f)	Buzimba
	(g)	Ngarama, Shema and Kashari
	(h)	Igara
	(i)	Buhweju
and	(j)	Bunyaruguru.[9]

During the next decade Ankole's territory was further modified. First, within the next few years, south-west Shema and south-west Igara were brought under the influence of the protectorate administration.[10] Next, in 1907, the chief of Bukanga placed himself under the administrative control of Ankole. For several decades henceforth, Bukanga continued to rank as a county. Meanwhile, Ankole 'lost' Kabula and Mawogola counties to Buganda, of which it was regretfully reminded even in 1962.[11] Similarly, Ankole's potential claims on Kitagwenda, which went to Toro, did not materialise. Ankole's external boundaries finally reached completion in 1914 when Kajara was added as a county.

These boundary rearrangements are significant for several reasons. One is the changed demographic basis that arose after Ankole's expansion. Within its traditional confines Nkore had been essentially a Bahima state; we saw that it was so notwithstanding the fact that many Bairu lived within its territory. Though they constituted a majority, most of these Bairu did not live in the core of the kingdom, but rather to the north, west and south of it. The central parts were given over to Bahima-controlled pastoralism. Moreover, as also noted, in Nkore Bahima constituted a larger minority than they did elsewhere in the interlacustrine origin.

The enlargement of Ankole crucially modified the relative numbers of Bairu and Bahima. Virtually all annexed areas, with the exception of Kajara, had known more overwhelming Bairu majorities than existed in Nkore. Igara had had a Bahima-based monarchy but otherwise a predominantly Bairu population. More pronouncedly, still, Buhweju's royalty was of Babito derivation (though by and large identifying itself with Bahima during the present century), while the rest of its population was Bairu. In Bunyaruguru there were no Bahima, though its agriculturalist population was not known as 'Bairu' (and would neither, in effect until today, call themselves 'Banyankore' – since in their conception Ankole's boundaries begin south at Igara). Parts of Shema, Rwampara and Mitoma had also known hardly any Bahima residents until colonial rule, or only relatively recently through encroachments from Mpororo. Only Kajara, therefore, which included another plains area, added any substantial number of Bahima to the expanded Ankole district.

As a result of these population distributions, there was a significant decrease of Bahima proportional to Bairu in Ankole, as opposed to Nkore. While earlier, as noted, Bahima may have constituted as much as 40 to 60 per cent of the population of Nkore, after its territorial expansion (and simultaneous epidemics and political upheavals)[12], the figure in Ankole was closer to 5 to 10 per cent. If it was thus remarkable that the Bahima stratum would nonetheless provide most of the administrative and political leadership, in terms of senior chieftaincies occupied in Ankole, this fact was even more striking considering that Bahima administrative rule during the colonial period for the first time extended directly to many Bairu communities.

Closely related is a second point of interest in Ankole's boundary changes. Nominally, all the incorporated areas were placed under the rulership of the Omugabe of Ankole, which should thus be remembered when considering the role of Ankole kingship in the present century. Evidently, from that moment on the Ankole dynasty had few traditional roots, if any, in more than half its domain. This does not necessarily mean that kingship per se was an alien element in incorporated areas. Several of the areas comprising Ankole exhibited significant similarities not only in terms of language and ways of life, but also in social organisation, including the institution of kingship. In historic times, the fluctuating balance of power had often caused rulership to change in the area, and as it had for long been expressed in Ankole, 'it does not matter who takes over, they are all kings'. Nonetheless, for a kingship which was to be put to the test of generating new meaning and functions, the lack of direct historical roots in a large section of its domain would doubtless make this task more difficult. In terms of its territorial jurisdiction, therefore, the Ankole monarchy found its traditional basis of legitimacy significantly reduced at the beginning of the century.

The reduction of Bahinda influence

Colonial transformation included various other developments which impinged upon the political structure in Ankole. Administrative impacts combined with basic economic, educational and religious effects profoundly to restructure the society, creating new sociopolitical categories and new sets of cleavages and alignments. These effects are particularly important for us in as far as they changed the role and composition of the new politico-administrative elite in the expanded district. Again, the early colonial period was one in which several baseline developments took place in this regard, determining the direction in which subsequent change would move.

One such development, which had direct implications for the position of the kingship, brought a pre-colonial rivalry to a direct bearing on the composition of the new Ankole elite. Once the colonial framework was established, a struggle for influence was waged on a clan basis between groups which aspired to positions of reward and privilege. The result of this was that, early in the century, the Ankole monarchy was put to a test by the elimination of a large part of its traditional entourage, the Bahinda clan, as a political force. The British entry led to the culmination and final decision of a long-standing rivalry between the Bahinda and the Bashambo. The Bahinda, it will be recalled, formed the royal clan of Nkore, whose members had exclusive title to the Obugabeship and to various senior chieftainships. The Bashambo were the royal clan of the neighbouring kingdom of Mpororo, of which parts were incorporated into Ankole at the time of British intervention.[13] Both were Bahima clans and stood in a similar relationship to the Bairu population in their respective areas.

In the nineteenth century, the Bashambo had been gaining ground as rulers in various other areas which came under the suzerainty of Ankole, and they thus had to be counted as a force of no small significance in the expanded Ankole kingdom. But not only did the Bahinda-Bashambo strife become increasingly salient due to the incorporation of annexed territories into Ankole; it was also directly related to the superimposition of colonial overrule. While the British had a golden opportunity to exploit this clan conflict to consolidate their power in Ankole, it was actually the Bashambo who readily took advantage of the British presence. As it turned out, however, their interest appeared to coincide largely with that of the British, so that the result might not have been very different if the British had taken the initiative to manipulate the clan conflict.

It is not surprising, therefore, that the struggle between Bahinda and Bashambo took a decisive turn precisely during the years which immediately followed the introduction of British overrule. From shortly before the signing of the Ankole Agreement in 1901, the Enganzi or principal chief in Ankole, was a Mushambo, Nuwa Mbaguta.[14] He remained on the scene almost as long as Kahaya, the then ruling Omugabe, namely until the late 1930s, but after an apparently cordial relationship during the first few years of their tenure, immediately around 1900, virtually the entire four decades which followed were marked by mutual rivalry and hostility. In the eyes of the British, Mbaguta was co-operative, interested in innovations, and eager to follow their instructions.

With their backing he asserted himself throughout as a shrewd and powerful potentate. From the point of view of protectorate officials, therefore, Mbaguta was the ideal kind of native authority to work with. Through him many administrative measures were introduced and implemented in Ankole, earning him many laudable commentaries in the records of British officers. As he was an effective and reliable instrument to make use of, the scope of his influence was in no small way promoted by the administration. Almost unnoticed, the office of Enganzi rose in accordance with the stature of the incumbent, imparting to Mbaguta a role unequalled by any of his predecessors. In fact, only one pre-1900 Enganzi seems to be vaguely remembered in Ankole, as against several generations of Abagabe.[15] And so, Mbaguta, the 'brightest star near the moon', as was the original meaning of the word 'Enganzi', came to eclipse even the Omugabe himself in actual influence.

Being an outsider to the traditional establishment of Ankole, Mbaguta was seen as a more neutral and manipulable agent of transformation than might otherwise have been the case. Being the leader of a clan which was engaged in continuous rivalry with the royal clan of Ankole, he was keen to exploit all possible opportunities to curtail Bahinda influence and to further Bashamho interests. As a key contact man of the British, several such chances offered themselves to him. The establishment of a colonial administration, which necessitated a considerable amount of accommodation on the part of the senior chiefs, largely Bahinda, was by far the major of these opportunities. The traditional chiefs were incorporated in an administrative command system which, notwithstanding its benefits, not only imposed specific duties but also implied considerable restrictions to their exercise of authority. The Bahinda chiefs soon felt that the objectives of bureaucratic control were encroaching much further upon their freedom than they wanted, and their reactions to these innovations accordingly varied between reluctance and resistance.

Early in the century this culminated in a series of incidents. Government officers were engaged in strong actions against Igumira, the leader of the discontented Bahinda, and his followers. For some years after the death of Ntare V in 1895, Igumira had been the strongest chief and virtual ruler of Nkore.[16] Upon the establishment of British control he was relegated to the position of a county chief and more generally found his influence severely curtailed. When these restrictions caused him to rebel, the British exiled him to Buganda, a measure for which Mbaguta deserves special credit. Many other chiefs were also dismissed during the early years of British rule. The effect of these measures was thus to leave Mbaguta's power virtually unchallenged among the Ankole elite. Many Bahinda took refuge in Buganda and elsewhere, an evacuation which was accelerated after the murder of a British officer, St Galt, in 1905. (The background of this murder has largely remained a mystery, although many people in Ankole believe that it originated directly from the Bahinda-Bashambo conflict.)[17]

While to date Ankole historiography has been surprisingly inexplicit or inconclusive about this episode, its importance is suggested by the fact that by far the larger part of the Bahinda aristocracy fled from Ankole out of fear of punitive sanctions by Mbaguta and the British. So widespread and lasting was this evacuation that it necessitated, in the 1930s, a special recruitment effort in Buganda to find an eligible Muhinda candidate to become a successor to the incumbent Omugabe. This was Gasyonga, virtually unknown in Ankole when he came back there, and with only a doubtful claim to the Obugabe.[18] The more immediate consequence of these developments, meanwhile, was that of the ranks of Bahinda only the Omugabe, Kahaya, and very few others remained in Ankole. A number of the positions which fell vacant were taken by Bashambo and other Bahima, and a good many chieftainships were filled by Baganda especially recruited by Mbaguta. Divorced from his Bahinda kinsmen, Kahaya thus came to stand rather isolated and, where possible, Mbaguta did not fail to by-pass him further.

Clearly, therefore, with the elimination of the Bahinda stratum an important departure from the traditional political structure was effected. Severance of the links with the Bahinda aristocracy was a source of strain and frustration especially for the Omugabe, as it deprived him both of the power structure and the traditional frame of reference that once defined his position in the system. The ties of patronage had been ruptured, and for political resources the Omugabe would need to turn elsewhere. Inevitably, the legitimacy of the kingship suffered. Had the Bahinda retained their influence in Ankole, a more prolonged conflict of conceptions of authoritative institutions, focusing particularly on the kingship, might have marked the years of colonial rule. As it was, the British design for the administration of Ankole did not meet an effective opposition after the initial abortive resistance, which made it all the more easy to implant. Basically, therefore, the Bahinda-Bashambo strife should be regarded as one which accelerated processes of colonial transformation, including the weakening of the institution of kingship.

Notes

1 The concept of 'franchise' may help to solve an apparent contradiction between external control and extensive chiefly powers. Colonial domination in many parts of the world was largely based on, and maintained through, a certain 'formula' for government and administration. While its execution was largely laid in the hands of local individuals and groups, strict adherence to the formula was continuously demanded. Among other things, this gave the system its near universalistic quality and made the pattern of organisation not incomparable to that of, e.g., the Roman Catholic church or some multi-national corporations.

2 This quality seems aptly illustrated by some of the counsel contained in the *Notes for Officers appointed to Uganda*, published by the Crown Agents for the Colonies, London, 1934. 'In Entebbe, Kampala and Jinja and the larger centres the population and facilities permit of most English games being pursued. Golf, cricket, tennis, soccer and occasionally rugger are played, and in the majority of out-stations there are tennis-courts and rough golf courses. If, however, in bush stations these facilities are entirely lacking, regular exercise should always be taken, such as a brisk walk or a stroll with a shot gun.' (p.19).

3 Uganda Protectorate, *Native Administration*, Entebbe, 1939) : 4. With its implied 'receptivity' of colonial rule, this statement does not quite describe the process as it took place in Ankole. Though in no way of the magnitude of the physical violence used in the subjugation of

Bunyoro, some instances of physical conquest occurred in Ankole, mainly involving some of the areas which were subjugated and incorporated into the expanded district. Cf. Tarsis B. Kabwegyere, 'The Dynamics of Colonial Violence: The Inductive System in Uganda', *The Journal of Peace Research*, IX, 4, 1972.
4   *Native Administration*, 5.
5   *Ankole Agreement*, 1901 para 3.
6   *Willis Journal*, 11:227-29.
7   Cf. *Daudi Ndibarema vs. Enganzi of Ankole*, Her Majesty's Court of Appeal for Eastern Africa, Civil Appeal No.78 of 1959.
8   The precolonial position has been summarised as follows in *East African Chiefs*:
    1. Isingiro, the old Kaaro-Karungi (the 'good land'), i.e. the nucleus of the kingdom of Nkore; 2. Shema, formerly part of the kingdom of Mpororo; 3. Rwampara, formerly part of the kingdom of Mpororo; 4. Nyabushozi, taken by conquest at the expense of Bunyoro; 5. Kashari, ditto; 6. Mitoma, ditto. To this core, the British added on their assumption of power : 7. Igara, a kingdom of similar status to Nkore until the mid-nineteenth century, when it became its tributary. This relationship was formalised by the British; 8. Buhweju, a kingdom that came into the sphere of influence of Nkore in the eighteenth century; 9. Bunyaruguru, an offshoot of the kingdom of Mpororo. (Stenning, 'The Nyankole': 156-57.) For a more detailed account of the expansion of the kingdom, see H.F. Morris, 'The Making of Ankole', *Uganda Journal*, XXI, 7, 1957: 204-07, and his, *A History of Ankole*.
9   It was also stipulated that these ten divisions did 'not include the whole area of the district of Ankole, but (that) those portions of the district which border more closely on the Congo Free State and German Territory will be subject to the same regulations as those set forth in this Agreement, and will for the present be administered by the principal European official placed in civil charge of the Ankole district, until such time as the chiefs thereof voluntarily place themselves under the suzerainty of Kahia.' Ankole Agreement, para. 2. (Kahia is an earlier spelling of Kahaya, the Omugabe of Ankole.)
10 Morris, *A History of Ankole*. p. 43.
11 E.g., 'Kabula and Mawogola counties should return to Ankole' (translated title), *Agetereine*, IV, 9, 27 April 1962: 7.
12 See below, on the population distribution, Mushanga (*op. cit.*, p. 29) estimates the Bairu to constitute 92-96 per cent of the total, the remainder being Bahima. Stenning similarly estimated the proportions of Bairu and Bahima to be 'about nine to one'. (Stenning, 'Salvation in Ankole': 258). Lukyn-Williams, on the other hand, estimated the proportions to be 14 to 1. F. Lukyn-Williams, 'Blood-brotherhood in Ankole (Omukago),' *Uganda Journal*, II, 1, 1934: 34.
13 See H. F. Morris, 'The Kingdom of Mpororo', *Uganda Journal*, XIX, 2, 1955:204-07, and Morris, *A History of Ankole* : 17-22.
14 F. Lukyn-Williams, 'Nuwa Mbaguta, Nganzi of Ankole', *Uganda Journal*, X, 2, 1946: 196-208.
15 The Enganzi was the above mentioned Muhigi. It should be noted, however, that the memory of past Abagabe appears to have fluctuated. Roscoe writes that when he first visited Ankole '...it was impossible to obtain from the people any information as to the name of their previous rulers', while later, it appeared to him, 'Contact with other tribes, especially with the Baganda and the Bakitara, (had) aroused a desire to have a genealogy of the royal family, and a list of kings was prepared'. Roscoe, *op.cit.*, 34. (Abagabe is the plural of Omugabe).
16 H. F. Morris, *A History of Ankole* :35.

17 A useful introduction of the puzzle is H. F. Morris, 'The Murder of H. St. Galt', *Uganda Journal* 24, 1, 1960: 1-15. Despite lengthy and minute inquiries, the background to this incident has long remained a mystery. In recent years, the view has been circulated that
the murder was a Bahinda plot to thwart Mbaguta's popularity with the British. The alleged murderer was a Mushambo who was himself found killed immediately following the Galt murder. Whether there was indeed an attempt to implicate Mbaguta by construing an incident for which the onus would come to lay on the Bashambo remains unproven, though its result was rather a strengthening of Mbaguta's position.
18 *Obugabe* is the Runyankore word for Ankole kingship.

4
The Redefinition of Kingship

Not the least important effect of colonialism in Ankole society was that which it had on the institution of kingship itself. As we have seen, the institution's incorporation into the colonial command structure, the reduction of the Omugabe's traditional entourage, the Bahinda, and the expansion of scale of Ankole at the establishment of British rule, all seriously affected the position of the kingship. Already, the context which was so redefined weakened its potential support in the society and reduced its chances of an adaptation which might have been in any way comparable to that shown in the case of some other monarchies. In addition, the colonial government drastically transformed the role of kingship itself. The basic fact that the continued existence of the institution came to depend on colonial policy led to major inroads into the authoritative and symbolic roles of Ankole kingship, eroding its traditional functions and causing it to lose its essential meaning.

For a proper perspective on this role transformation the ingredients of the traditional system should be kept in mind. Structurally, we saw that the system was characterised by dispersed powers and a high degree of collective decision-making – mostly among and for Bahima – while normatively it featured strongly hierarchical values about authority.[1] Moreover, these aspects were significantly interconnected, since the hierarchical values made sense primarily in relation to the participatory style of decision making. In this context, there was a central focus on the institution of kingship, whose role was of critical significance. The colonial government fundamentally changed these characteristics and their interconnections. It could not tolerate an institution with any measure of autonomy, but sought to make it a mouthpiece of colonial policy. The kingship was fitted into the bureaucratic structure and in time the institution was adorned with a thick overlay of new ceremonialism. As a result, new distinctions developed between the ideal and the actual powers of kingship. But contrary to the historical example, these lacked any complementarity and what would finally emerge was rather a caricature of the traditional institution, accelerating the erosion of supportive sentiments it had once inspired.

The key to this development was that the employment of traditional authority entailed some profound ambiguities which were to seriously threaten its effectiveness. Even if some early European administrators had a passing interest in the exotic, or took a delight in exploring the role and meaning of historic kingship, in the day-to-day execution of tasks. They commonly assessed traditional authority mainly in terms of its command over the popular will or the obedience it might be able to provide. The assumption was that 'all you could in fact do was to explain what you wanted to some "Native Authority"; and as he – or she – was generally only too anxious to please, the result was usually that it was done.'[2] Thus, in British eyes, the role of the kingship was viewed as one that should secure a traditional fiat for the execution of colonial policies. It required that, in the eyes of the population, the legitimacy of traditional authority had to be maintained if it was to remain effective.

But, in those early days, to treat a king or chief with all the pomp and protocol which later became more common might have stimulated a renewed consciousness and taste for actual authority on their part; this could easily have come to conflict with the conduct of regular colonial administration and could by no means be allowed. Obviously, therefore, there was a fragile balance if not tension between the requirements of continued legitimacy and external control, and it is not difficult to imagine that the subtleties of the compromise may somehow have escaped a man like the Omugabe of Ankole. He was told time and again that he was supreme chief or 'Kabaka'. Moreover, there was the fresh memory of the traditional period in which his position, as we have seen, was indeed symbolically exalted.[3] Yet the tendency was clearly to employ him as an instrument with which to gain popular acceptance for administrative measures. An incongruous element in the new bureaucratic edifice, he was, in effect, ordered around by British officers to explain colonial policies and to induce compliance among the people of Ankole.

Ambiguities were especially noticeable in regard to the Omugabe's position vis-a-vis the administrative chiefs. For long these relationships were not explicitly laid down and, moreover, the official line in respect of these matters tended to change over time. The policy was evidently to have it both ways, that is, to keep full control over the chiefs in the hands of the district administration while adhering to the idea that all authority was exercised in the name and under the supervision of the Omugabe. In a way the arrangement was reminiscent of a framework of constitutional monarchy in which government functions are carried out under a symbolic umbrella of monarchical authority. But the pattern's novelty in the Ankole sociopolitical context, the ambiguity with which it was employed and, above all, the fact that colonial officers as a third, 'supra' party controlled the system's 'executive' and 'symbolic' components, made the arrangement fundamentally different from patterns of constitutional monarchy in the conventional sense.

The practice to which the arrangement was put illustrated these differences. Chiefs of counties and lower divisions were appointed by and held responsible to the district administration.[4] District officials inspected their books, kept records of their administrative performance, and reported on their diligence in implementing bye-laws. Yet the Omugabe was put forward as their superior, and this was done in more than a purely nominal sense. From the British point of view, it seemed practicable to make use of his influence over the subordinate chiefs. For this, however, he somehow had to be given an opportunity to display his authority. The Omugabe was therefore also asked to tour and inspect and report. Clearly, this entailed some problems, of which the duplication of supervision was only the least. For one thing, the standards of good administration entertained by the Omugabe were not necessarily the same as those of British officials and as a result differences almost inevitably arose. Chiefs would either find themselves confronted with two kinds of demand and possibly be unable to decide which to give priority, or the Omugabe might follow the official line and communicate directives which he himself did not quite accept.[5] Moreover, the relationship between the Omugabe and the chiefs was entirely different to that in the pre-colonial situation.

The Omugabe became part of an administrative command system and it was expected that his traditional legitimacy would ease his assumption of this new role. But because this legitimacy was associated with an earlier and different authority relationship, the new role was not an instant success; instead, it puzzled and embarrassed the Omugabe as well as the chiefs. Moreover, as the exact scope of his authority had been left exceedingly vague, the chances of a successful learning process were all the more problematic. Finally, to function effectively in any capacity within the district organisation, a certain amount of administrative proficiency was a *sine qua non*. The whole system was designed on the basis of paperwork and bureaucratic codes, and whoever did not master their essentials was at a loss. No wonder that the Omugabe, who was wholly untrained for these purposes, should have felt a sense of inadequacy in discharging the administrative tasks devolved upon him. Rather more surprising is that the problems created by this situation were not readily appreciated by British officials; it was only as late as 1938, when the Omugabe asked for copies of reports to be sent to him, that a district commissioner began to wonder 'Has the Omugabe facilities for starting a filing system of his own?'[6]

These ambiguities and contradictions led to increasingly strained relationships between the Omugabe and British officials. Lack of interest in and resentment of the British administration came more and more to characterise the Omugabe's attitude, and a vicious circle ensued in which growing impatience and irritation on the part of colonial officers and increasing apathy and surliness on the part of the Omugabe were some of the more salient elements. Painstaking reporters of everything happening within their jurisdiction, colonial administrators have left an extensive record of these difficulties. A letter sent on 3 March 1907, by the acting collector in Mbarara to the sub-commissioner, Western province, reporting one instance of friction with the Omugabe, deserves to be quoted at length as it typifies the attitude and tone of the earlier administrators towards the Omugabe:

Sir,

I have the honour to report that Kahaya, Kabaka of Ankole was yesterday guilty of conduct of such an unseen nature that I feel that it should be brought to your notice.

This consisted in misbehaviour towards myself and insolence of such a sort that it should in my opinion be recorded. The immediate and apparent cause of this lapse upon his part was that I found it necessary to speak somewhat seriously to Kahaya with respect to the manner in which he treated certain requests I made to him in connection with the arrangements for the Anglo-Congolese Commission. My reproofs which were certainly not more severe than the occasion demanded were received by Kahaya in a spirit of mixed sullenness and impertinence. He informed me that he could see that I wanted to quarrel with him, that he would henceforth refuse to visit me if sent for, and that he would not attempt to carry out my requests. Thinking that he had momentarily lost control of himself I endeavoured for a space to remonstrate with him. But he either maintained an obstinate silence, or replied with sullen impertinence. Seeing that further conciliatoriness could serve no useful purpose, I told him that I would tolerate his tone no longer, I told him that he had been grossly impertinent to me, and that I would see that his behaviour was reported. I then ordered him to leave my house, and not to return until he could behave himself.

Kahaya has not of course adhered to the wild statements above described. He received my Interpreter within two hours of the occurrence, and gave directions that what I required should be attended to. And he has today met an inquiry from me as to whether he will come to see me in a proper manner, in a becoming spirit. And did this outbreak of temper stand by itself I should not give to it much heed. For Kahaya is liable to fits of extreme and hasty temper, joined at times with an ineradicable obstinacy. I have seen him before quite inarticulate with rage against Baguta. But the whole trend of his conduct of late, and his normal demeanour when any attempt has been made to guide him or to induce him to regard seriously the responsibilities of his position compel me to think that we need to be very careful in our treatment of Kahaya. During the past few weeks in particular I have been very dissatisfied with his manner and conduct. And because two weeks ago I thought fit to censure him for repeating to me five days in succession a statement which he knew to be a deliberate falsehood, he used language which if taken seriously would seem to indicate that in his opinion the Kabaka could not be found fault with by the Collector.

This is of course an attitude which cannot be allowed for a moment. It is needless to say that it will be a bad thing for Ankole if Kahaya and the Bahima Chiefs in general are allowed to persist in the notion, which they undoubtedly entertain, and have cherished for some time, that specious promises are all that is required, and that performance is scarcely even expected; it will be worse if the idea gains ground that the Collector can always be put off by perfunctory excuses, and will not venture upon strong remonstrances. The Bahima will need wise handling.

                I have the honour to be,
                      Sir,
                Your most obedient humble Servant.

In this instance, the sub-commissioner in turn communicated the incident to his superiors at Entebbe, adding that 'it would appear from it that Kahaya's character is not even now formed and he should be treated to discipline much as a school boy,' and concluding that 'he will have to be properly kept in his place.'[7] Accordingly, he instructed the acting collector that:

> [Kahaya] must learn that the Collector is the representative of the Government in his Country and any disrespect shown to him, or other Government Officers, is a slight which will not be lightly passed over. Please also inform him that I have reported the matter to His Excellency the Commissioner and make a note of the occurrence in your record book of Chiefs' characters.'[8]

A few days after the incident, the acting collector was proud to report that Kahaya had visited him again and that 'his behaviour on this occasion was all that could be desired'. 'But I venture to think,' he went on, that 'every opportunity should be available to cause Kahaya to realise more clearly his responsibilities as Kabaka, and the attitude it is deemed to assume towards a Collector and towards Europeans in general.'[9]

The problem was not quite solved, however, and over the following decades a long series of reprimands reached the Omugabe. In 1921, for instance, the district commissioner of Ankole issued a warning to the Omugabe in the following terms:

> I notice that these days you never seem to go to the Lukiiko or take part in the work of your country, why is this so? Your people are complaining that their Head Chief is no longer there to look after them. You must realise that it is your duty to preside at the Meetings and Courts of the Lukiiko, and not allow other people to take away your power, so I hope that it will not be necessary for me to have to write again about this.[10]

A few years later, a letter from the provincial commissioner to the Omugabe conveyed the same concern:

> 1. I am informed by the District Commissioner, Ankole, that you are taking little or no interest in the Administration of your country. 2. I hope when I visit Ankole in December that I shall find you have been attending Lukiiko regularly and are trying your best to help on the country of which you are the Omugabe. 3. If you consider you are so ill that you can no longer carry out your duties, would you like to retire on a pension and have your successor appointed now.[11]

Again, in 1933, after visiting the Omugabe, a district commissioner wrote in his report:

I explained that I was very dissatisfied with him as Mugabe and that Europeans at Mbarara, Fort Portal and Entebbe were saying that he was useless and was no good. He had spoilt his name among them and now he was spoiling his name among his own people... I told him that I wished to help him and wished to uphold the Mugabeship for the good of the country, but I could do nothing if he did not help me. [12]

In that same year, the Omugabe was also reminded:

> Always remember that a Mugabe who does not see his people and to whom they cannot come is not worthy of the post of Mugabe or pay.[13]

And on 31 December 1937, the district commissioner wrote to all local heads of departments to express his 'regret that the disrespect shown by the Mugabe made it impossible for me to hold Lukiiko'.

It had also become apparent that the Omugabe's behaviour conflicted in several ways with the codes for prudence and propriety introduced by the British. In 1926, for instance, the Omugabe was told by the provincial commissioner that:

> The Government wish to accomplish two matters, namely. (1) to make such suitable arrangements as will prevent your money being taken wrongly by other people without your knowledge, as is happening now, (2) by a proper system of supervision and accounting to prevent your having debts beyond your income and seeing that all such debts are paid every month thus preventing disgrace coming both on yourself and on your country. You are at liberty to spend all your money as you like and we do not wish to inquire as to how you spend it provided you do not get into debt and agree to the supervision that the Government think necessary.[14]

And in 1927, the provincial commissioner instructed the officer-in-charge at Mbarara:

> As regards the Omugabe, will you please convey the following remarks to him :
> (a) It is the business of the Omugabe to understand any rules made with regard to his country, and that if he is mentally unable of understanding them he is not fit to be Omugabe.
> (b) That there is a legal order limiting the amount of beer to be brewed, and that he the Omugabe is guilty of an offence and liable to severe punishment for instructing people to break the law.
> (c) That it is the aim and object of the Government to prevent drunkenness and that his action is calculated to encourage it and is therefore contrary to Government orders to chiefs and that such action cannot be tolerated.

(d) That he the Omugabe is not above the law of the country and that if he cannot obey the law and the instructions of the Government, I will place the matter before His Excellency the Governor with a view to considering his removal.

(e) That this is by no means the first adverse report received on his conduct, and that unless an improvement is noted, drastic action will have to be taken.[15]

Various other irregularities, big and small, likewise occupied the attention of colonial officers. On 16 August 1921, the district commissioner felt compelled to write to the provincial commissioner 'I report that it is my duty to bring to your notice a serious scandal complicating the Omugabe, Katikiro and the Sekibobo.'[16] The 'scandal' involved the queen of Ankole, and in the instructions which followed she was to be escorted by 'reliable men' to Mbarara. On 16 September 1926, renewed disappointments caused the acting provincial commissioner to communicate to the officer-in-charge, Ankole, that he was 'directed to convey to the Omugabe an expression of His Excellency the Governor's surprise and regret that he – the Omugabe – as head of the Native Government in Ankole, should have committed irregularities in connection with the collection of grazing fees in contravention of his own Lukiko Funds.' And in 1935, according to the Ankole district annual report for that year, it was decided to cancel the Omugabe's game and elephant licence and to withdraw all privileges for five years, owing to his 'infringement of the Game Laws'.

In response to these injunctions and reprimands, the Omugabe made occasional promises to improve his conduct and meet the standards set for him by the protectorate administration. The psychological intimidation to which he was subject at the hands of colonial officers thus began to have its intended effects: the Omugabe increasingly posed and acted as the 'schoolboy', in need of tutelage by his British superiors, which he was so often made out to be. One such pledge to 'behave himself' is contained in a letter he wrote in 1927 to the district commissioner: [17]

> Dear Sir,
>
> I have seen the P.C.'s letter No. 694/395, which he wrote warning me that I should do my work for my country. Now I am writing to inform you what I am going to do in future, I expect to make a big Safari rounding the District like the Katikiro has recently done, my principal work on my Safari is to see the chiefs' work and encourage them also to encourage the Bakopi (peasants) to cultivate lot of food for famine.
>
> After coming back from the Safari I will preside (sit) in the Lukiko regularly, so I hope in that case I may be able to abolish my present habit of sitting in my house doing nothing. I confirm this before you that I will do my best to do the Administration work as it is required by both the Government Officers and my people, and in future there will be no more slackness in me. I shall be very

grateful if you will kindly write to the P.C. W.P. and inform him that his warning has been strictly carried out, and that I will not cause more trouble in future. My safari will start from here on the 15th inst. I hope to come and see you in your office tomorrow morning at 9 a.m. and will talk to you about my Safari, etc.
              I beg to remain,
              Sir
              Your Obedient Servant, E. S. Kahaya, Omugabe

Some such statements of intent actually inaugurated a renewed involvement of the Omugabe in public affairs. He would then do some touring and address audiences on the objectives of government policy, acting as the mouthpiece of the administration. In a speech given by the Omugabe to the Bahima in 1940, for instance, the topics covered included:

1 want to remind you about important words which the Honourable Provincial Commissioner, Western Province, told you yesterday. He told you that in former days you were brave and clever people but when you got rich, you received other people to work for you, and little by little you became lazy and good for nothing.
2. ...the Government will help you in keeping cattle and making good butter and hides, so that they may be of good quality and good price. She will build a School here, but you must send to it your children and pay school fees for them.
3. Don't willingly break rules given to you by the Veterinary Officer. The well is made for you as a sample of good will, and you will make new ones by yourselves when this spoilt.
4. The Government will build a Hospital for you, but please do send to it your patients and have confidence in the Government Doctor rather than in your pagan witches.
5. In my last safari to Nyabushozi, I spoke to you about Poll Tax, I want now to remind you of the use of it. Money collected from poll tax is for use in: making roads, building hospitals and other buildings of chiefs, paying chiefs and all government porters.[18]

When asked to do so by the district officials and in his sporadic moments of involvement, the Omugabe might also call his subordinates to their duties. In respect to a chief's behaviour, for example, Kahaya reported to the district commissioner :

Sir, I have the honour to inform you that I have seen Mr. Firimoni Lwaigambwa Mugyema, and reproved him for his drunkenness, and I have instructed him to cease drinking native beer. He has agreed to my advice, and he has sworn in my presence that he will never drink it again.[19]

Such an intervention, made towards the end of his rulership, was surely becoming behaviour for an Omugabe in His Majesty's service. And it was in that commendable spirit that Kahaya's successor, Gasyonga, expressed himself when taking over in 1944. Thanking the governor for his recognition, he wrote, '1 assure Your Excellency that with the advice of the Protectorate Government and the Ankole Native Administration I shall endeavour to be one of His Majesty's Loyal Servants.'[20]

Perceptions of role conflict

The point of interest in the reports we have seen is that they offer some insight into the highly problematic relationship between the Omugabe of Ankole and British administrative officers. Not only do the communications of these officials tell us something about the areas of friction. But a certain official viewpoint emerges from the records. This viewpoint is of particular interest to us. Basically the notion entertained by district provincial commissioners as well as other colonial officers appears to have been that the Omugabe did not know his place and did not know his role. They found that he lacked understanding of and interest in the tasks assigned to him. And from the tenor of the remarks they submitted, it is apparent that British officials tended to attribute the difficulties in dealing with the Omugabe largely to the make-up of his personality. He was considered physically and intellectually weak, sullen, lacking in will and moral acumen. Virtually throughout the reign of the Omugabe Kahaya, that is until 1944, this was the most common and favoured explanation. Accordingly, in the series of annual district reports for Ankole, the sections concerning the Omugabe together read like a long temperature chart on his condition as the following entries illustrate:

1934	'The outstanding feature of the year has been the new lease of life that the Mugabe has taken. I indicated the possibility of this revival at the end of last year.'	
1935	'The interest of the Mugabe in the affairs of the District has been but sporadic.'	
1936	'Much the same comment applies to the Omugabe as in previous years, namely that on the pretext of ill-health he confines himself to his house and takes but little interest in the affairs of the District.'	
1937	'The shortness of my time in Ankole make it difficult to pass comment on the activities of the Mugabe and Chiefs.'	
1938	'The Omugabe broke his leg during the year but though it has not completely recovered he has during the last quarter been able to go on tour.'	
1939	'The Mugabe made two tours during the year and appeared interested in all activities of his people. His health was precarious but mentally he was able to deal with all matters referred to him.'	

1940	'The Omugabe made one extended tour during which he visited several Saza headquarters. He continued to take an intelligent interest in all the activities of the district.'
1941	'The Mugabe toured Nyabushozi county and addressed the Bahima in a forlorn attempt to make them help in the development of their new Saza and to stop emigration to Buganda. He has been sick during the last three months of the year.'
1942	'The Mugabe has remained in bad health during the whole year. His only public appearance was at the time of the visit of the S.A.A.F. when he attended the display.'[21]
1943	'The Mugabe has continued in bad health and has made no public appearance during the year.'
1944	'In October the District was shocked to hear of the death of the Omugabe, E. S. Kahaya II. He has been in bad health for some considerable time and had taken little or no part in the administration of the district.'[22]

In considering this chronicle, it seems fair to assume that Kahaya was a man of limited physical powers and of no spectacular intellectual resources. Nowhere, in British or local accounts does he emerge as a man of great vision or foresight, or as someone who would have his own will and stand by it. Of weak health and described by his early European visitors as 'a very stout overgrown youth' about whom there was nothing particularly regal',[23] his involvement was by and large a passive one; generally he tended to withdraw from the complexities with which he became surrounded from all sides, and these not merely British.

However, to explain problems in the relationship with the Omugabe simply by reference to personality factors appears not only superficial, it too easily shifts the onus from the structural arrangements he came to operate in and the way in which these were manipulated by the British. The ambiguity of his role made misunderstandings and conflict practically unavoidable, and there is every reason to believe that the problems would have been even more serious had the Omugabe had a stronger personality.[24] Kahaya was a boy of about 18 when he was installed, almost immediately before the British made their entry. Hence, the conception of his office, or the lack of it, was largely British-derived; if there were difficulties, these were inherent in the very definition of his role.

Long after the early days of self-confident colonialism had passed, British officers developed a more balanced understanding of the structural transitions they had enacted. As Mitchell reflected in 1939:

> Few of us realised ... that the instrument which we were using could not retain its effectiveness if we deprived it – as we generally did – of most of its powers and responsibilities, to say nothing of its revenues. I have often wondered since those

early days that the Chiefs thought it worthwhile even to try to carry out our wishes, when we had taken from them the power to punish and often looked upon the tribute and service from their people, without which they could not exist, as being corrupt extortion.[25]

This contradiction was fully apparent in the instance of Ankole. The frequency with which the institution of kingship was used to induce compliance with administrative policies was inversely related to its actual usefulness for that purpose; accordingly, its employment tended to produce ever more marginal results.

For some time it was evidently felt that if only the Omugabe could be interested in the innovations proposed by the district administration, it would not be difficult to get the rest of the population to follow suit. However, the result was very different, not least because the role designed for the Omugabe was as foreign to the Banyankore as it was to the man himself. As contrived by the British administration, the role of the Omugabe departed in major ways from pre-colonial conceptions. This was not only because the Omugabe became subordinate to protectorate officials, but the idea of a bureaucratic line of command was also highly unfamiliar. The meaning of the institution in traditional times, which was to symbolise the political integration of a pluralistic polity through the hierarchical authority values associated with it, was irretrievably deflated by the use made of kingship to get acceptance for immediate ends.

This policy had assumed the existence of sources of actual power which the Omugabe had never had. It had further assumed that, whatever the original basis of his prestige, this would be prolonged within the new context to be established. Both these assumptions proved fallacious; when the Omugabe was asked to convey colonial policies to his people, they saw him perform in a capacity which made little sense either in the old or in the new framework. Even his relatively rare visits to various areas were felt as a burden and nuisance by the people concerned, as was evidenced in repeated complaints over the requirements to lay on food supplies for him and his retinue. Increasingly, therefore, he was met by lack of understanding and interest, which only enhanced his own uninterest and discomfort with his role, and ultimately led to the state of apathy and withdrawal which disappointed so many of his British superiors.

Kahaya did not possess the strong personality necessary to counter these trends, and his successor Gasyonga's case perhaps was not altogether different. But, again, had their demeanour been more powerful, friction might well have been much greater. The erosion of kingship, which, even if unintended, was the inevitable conclusion of the process of bureaucratisation, might then have been considerably complicated and delayed (or else speeded up by open conflict).

It should be clear that these points are not necessarily supportive of the view held by some anthropologists that, for an innovation to be successful, it must be hooked on to traditional cultural patterns.[26] On the contrary, new situations generate new orientations and values, and may well demand new structural adaptations. Even if the conditions under which some new structures are introduced may be questionable, institutional change is bound to occur wherever there is any juxtaposition of new and old elements. But to assume that an institution such as kingship can be drastically transformed while popular orientations and allegiances toward it will remain unaffected is profoundly misleading. The attempt to make use of the traditional role of kingship in Ankole was based on this ambiguity; far-reaching changes were introduced while assuming that the orientations which supported the old relationships would prevail. The structural transformations introduced in Ankole could ultimately lead only to obsolescence of the monarchy. Indeed, the redundancy of Ankole kingship was very much a built-in consequence of its use as a tool in the colonial machinery.

Colonial transformations and orientations towards kingship

Incorporated into the Uganda framework and with its territorial scale considerably expanded through annexations, we have seen that the Ankole monarchy's institutional role and set-up were subject to drastic changes during colonial times. Still, the various impacts we have noted did not exhaust the forces which led to a redefinition of the kingship. Besides rearranging the institution itself, policies of colonial control and transformation brought major changes in Ankole's social context, which, though more indirect in their effects, were hardly less consequential for the position of the monarchy. Colonial transitions caused significant reorientations of popular attitudes, not the least of which was a growing indifference towards the kingship. Inevitably, these developments could not but lead to a further erosion of the institution's role in Ankole society.

To appreciate these effects, we must return to the Bairu-Bahima division and pay special attention to the changing relationships between the two population groups. In doing so, one point in particular will need to be recalled. If in the pre-colonial period Bairu and Bahima had coexisted as largely distinct communities, though with Bahima preponderantly involved in the Nkore state system and with a variety of economic and political contacts across the two groups, an elementary but key consequence of colonial rule was the creation of a single administrative network for the whole area. Within this, socio-political relationships and orientations were increasingly directed towards a central focus and arena. Through the sheer operation of the colonial administration and their involvement in it, the tendency thus was for the Bairu and Bahima communities to become more closely drawn into, and part of, a single sociopolitical unit than they had been before.

But if such a tendency lay very much in the logic of developments, a less inevitable departure, as noted earlier, was the fact that Bahima were recruited in disproportionately large numbers into the senior ranks of the colonial administration. As it turned out, from the beginning of the century onwards, colonial rule for a long time sustained an ethnically restricted composition of the Ankole ruling stratum.

The situation which thus originated, and whose repercussions were later manifested in ethnic conflict, was essentially a colonial creation. What remains debatable is whether this was an unwitting or a deliberate creation. Both possibilities seem quite plausible and deserve some brief exploration.

The situation may have been unwittingly created if indeed the British erroneously based their policy on an understanding of history which assumed the existence of a rigid ethnic hierarchy in Nkore, with Bahima the rulers and Bairu the ruled. Several factors might support this possibility: the fact that the British entry was effected through contact with the Bahima, the difficulty of establishing the historical meaning, let alone the position, of 'Bairu' in Nkore society[27], and possibly the belief that hierarchy and subordination were given in all societies. As for the latter, the fact that four decades later the distinction between states and stateless systems should have been received as a major landmark in the scholarship and understanding of African society might confirm the long standing prevalence of such a belief.[28]

Nonetheless, the possibility that the policy of differential ethnic recruitment in Ankole was deliberate, intended to secure the support of one strategic section of the population so as to control more effectively the whole, deserves serious attention in the light of colonial practices elsewhere in Africa. Examples abound, but in two that were quite close to the Uganda scene, Burundi and the Sudan, the Belgians and British respectively placed members of one section (Batutsi; northerners) in a position of greater political supremacy over another (Bahutu; southerners) than they had known before.

In Uganda itself the point is illustrated by the employment of Baganda agents to help subjugate and rule annexed territories which constituted such an important ingredient of British strategies for control in Uganda. Some elements of this policy were even present in Ankole, though by and large the function of the Baganda chiefs recruited to the district turned out to be supportive of the new Bahima establishment. Meanwhile, the nominal authority given to the Ankole monarchy over various smaller entities amalgamated with the kingdom might itself also be seen as an expression of this 'unite and rule' approach.

These different possible explanations for the creation of an ethnically tiered administration do not necessarily exclude one another: those who established the colonial system in Ankole may have erred in their grasp of history but nonetheless also may have been determined to use ethnic divisions as a means of control. What matters is that beyond the question of the exact causes and calculations that intervened, for purposes of administering Ankole, the British clearly put their cards on the Bahima. Nor should it be overlooked in this connection that they were highly impressed with the Bahima: early reporters were nearly unanimous in their praise for the pastoralists' qualities, calling them 'born rulers' or a 'superior race'. Thus, for example, Johnston expressed as his view that '...the men of Hima blood are born gentlemen and one is so struck with their handsome bearing and charming manners as to desire ardently that this fine race may not come to extinction,'[29], thereby advancing opinions which in all probability no Muhima had asked for.

In the process, however, a more rigid and divisive ethnic cleavage was created than had existed before. Basically, the Bairu were treated as a subject category, the Bahima as an elite. For this the policy also provided its own justification; the appointment of Bahima to the senior chieftainships entailed a self-fulfilling hypothesis, namely that the Ankole polity (also implying precolonial Nkore) had 'always' been so constituted. These appointments soon obliterated any traces to the contrary – that is, not that Bahima had not been chiefs, but that they had been directly involved with and in control of the Bairu communities. That the theory proved persuasive can be gathered from subsequent literature on Ankole: most writers have accepted it for fact and proceeded with their reportage.

The reverse side of the coin was inevitably that Bairu for many years had only a chance of attaining the lower ranks of the chiefly hierarchy, a situation which was not changed by the withdrawal of the Bahinda chiefs and the new recruitments this necessitated. Instead, the staffing of these positions with other Bahima and with Baganda not only seemed to confirm that Bairu were considered ineligible to fill them, but for a prolonged period closed these ranks to them.

The significance of these arrangements should be measured not merely by the perquisites and the status which these offices entailed, however important they were to the individuals (and their retinue) concerned. In the context of colonial Uganda, they above all meant the power to control others, even if its exercise was kept within the bounds of formal jurisdictions. Through most of the colonial period this power extended over widely different areas, as wide as the notion of law and order could be stretched and thus in effect implied broad and pervasive domination over large population groups. But in a case where power was largely exercised over one ethnic group while it lay in the hands of members of another, such an arrangement had particularly severe implications for the structure of society.

It appears from the record that the Bahima establishment was given a fair amount of leeway in matters of recruitment, and that Mbaguta's role was especially influential.[30] Nor should one probably have expected this to be otherwise. During the early phases of British occupation colonial officers inevitably would have experienced acute problems in identifying alternative, meritorious candidates. Consequently, the pattern initially approximated one of co-optation, with the tacit approval of colonial officers. The Bahima elite thus could feel they were in control, as in a sense they were. But what perhaps they little realised (with the possible exception of some of the Bahinda who opted out) was that the control they exercised was itself a means of control for other objectives, the policies of British colonialism.

This approach to colonial administration through 'franchise' required a minimum of overseas investments and personnel, and in that sense was effective and economical. But its low expenditure was more than offset by the social costs inflicted upon the society. The policy of 'indirect rule' in the case of Ankole meant that one section of the population was set over and against the rest, thus creating a profound, and lasting, divisiveness which negatively affected sociopolitical relationships. Ironically, while the costs of colonial administration were thus 'internalised', it nonetheless placed the colonial power in a role of 'arbiter' of local conflicts. During a later period, especially the late fifties and early sixties, the various sides presented grievances about the opposite group to British officials and institutions, not fully realising that the pattern of their conflicts resulted largely from the way in which colonial policies had been inserted. It suggests that Ankole (or much of Uganda for that matter) might well have emerged as a more unified and vigorous society had the British undertaken the tasks of colonial administration in a more direct manner.

In the light of colonial policies and their effects, it is thus not surprising that a crucial element bearing on the destiny of the Ankole kingship centred on the Bairu-Bahima division. While in the pre-colonial era Bairu and Bahima had had different orientations to the monarchy, in order to preserve its legitimacy the monarchy would have needed to 'equalise' the symbolic identification of its ethnic 'constituents' and give Bairu and Bahima a sense of shared involvement in the kingship. This requirement, however, ran counter to colonial policy and its implied 'premise of inequality'. Ankole's evolving ethnic stratification, as it turned out, imposed an additional limitation on rejuvenation of kingship.

As the monarchy was being restyled, Bairu and Bahima simultaneously developed divergent attitudes toward the office, which, in a sense, led to a replication of earlier divergencies. Although the Bahima maintained a close identification with the monarchy, the source of this identification changed considerably. The Bairu, on the other hand, had never been very closely related to the monarchy, and when the institution lapsed into obsolescence, their reaction was one of growing indifference. There was also another strand of opinion among Bairu, however. As the monarchy was identified with Bahima overrule, its legitimacy was questioned at the same time that Bahima supremacy was challenged by Bairu. So, far from promoting the unification of ethnic segments through their joint identification with kingship, the Obugabe became a symbol of increasing tension between Bairu and Bahima.

The rise of ethnic hostility was the concomitant of a restratification process which became increasingly manifest towards the terminal years of colonial rule. While following the Ankole Agreement the principle of ethnic inequality had been variously reaffirmed and strengthened,[31] colonial rule also prompted social developments that increasingly caused the Bairu to question not only specific discriminatory practices but the whole rationale behind the 'premise of inequality'. The effect of modern education was to instil egalitarian orientations and aspirations among an increasing number of Bairu, a growing sense of dissatisfaction over their status as 'second-class citizens'. Bairu also developed an awareness of greater self-sufficiency from their mastery of modern skills, as well as from the new sources of income made available to them through the cultivation and sale of cash crops. The result of all this was the emergence in the 1940s and 1950s of a Bairu-led and Bairu-inspired protest movement which formalised and intensified the claims of Bairu to a fuller participation in Ankole affairs. Owing to this pressure, increased Bairu participation in the political life of Ankole was in fact forthcoming. But this was a slow process, and the relations between Ankole's ethnic groups were consequently marked by prolonged hostility.[32]

If the monarchy became a focal point of conflict, this was not so much the result of its own doing as a reflection of intensified ethnic antagonisms. These occurred at a time when the influence of the Obugabe was at its lowest ebb, and when the new functions vested in the Omugabe seemed strangely reminiscent of the emperor's new clothes. In contrast with the situation in adjacent Rwanda, the monarchy in Ankole was too weak to become a significant factor in the ethnic strife; yet ethnic rivalry was bound to occur at some point, and if for no other reason than to strengthen their respective claims, the contestants could scarcely resist the temptation of politicising the issue of monarchical legitimacy. To the Bairu, kingship was a constant reminder of Bahima claims to hegemony. Whatever pronouncements the Omugabe made to the effect that all Banyankore were equally his subjects,[33] these were inevitably received with a sense of strong disbelief by educated Bairu elements. As Bairu protest became increasingly vociferous during Gasyonga's reign, the latter's attitude became the target of growing criticisms on their part. Even though they knew that the kingship no longer had any direct influence in politics, any semblance of involvement of the Omugabe with Bahima tactics was invariably denounced by the Bairu as 'proof' of ethnic favoritism.

To the Bahima, the monarchy also became a symbol in a new political sense. Traditionally, the kingship symbolised, and in a way ensured, their political unity. Although the practical utility of the institution was now very much in doubt, the Omugabe's continued presence in office during a time of ethnic confrontation nonetheless strengthened Bahima feelings of identity and security. As they sensed the threats posed to their political supremacy, most Bahima sought to reverse the trend as best they could given the political resources available to them. From the 1940s, tension focused particularly on the number of senior chieftainships occupied by Bahima, as the displacement of Bahima chiefs inevitably meant a loss of resources, power and status for the group as a whole. While the ethnic distribution of these posts changed slowly, in the long run the numerically weaker Bahima were bound to suffer a decline of their privileged political status. Though forced to relinquish their position of pre-eminence, the Bahima derived a sense of unity and continued recognition from the conviction that the kingship was still 'theirs'. That this conviction was largely illusory is beside the point. Precisely because they were victims of this illusion, they failed to realise the full extent of their eclipse as a political elite, a fact which also helps to explain their relative quiescence during the transition. The retention of the monarchy through the period of ethnic restratification has thus probably smoothed the reversal of ethnic status in Ankole.

Somewhat anti-climactically, the contrasting attitudes of Bairu and Bahima almost never led to explicit demands for either the abolition or the retention of the Ankole monarchy. Several factors tended to mitigate ethnic tension and hence diminished the degree to which the monarchy became an issue in the dispute. One such factor was related to Ankole's status as a sub-system of Uganda. The essential point to note in this connection is that the national arena offered alternative avenues for upward social mobility for both Bairu and Bahima to those available in Ankole proper. Many of the best qualified Banyankore found employment in other parts of Uganda; while slowing down local competition for positions, this also helped to attenuate ethnic tension. For this reason intergroup conflict in Ankole never assumed the global proportions that it did in the ethnically stratified but closed system of Rwanda.[34] Nor did the survival of kingship become an all-pervasive issue, as in Rwanda.

Another explanation for the staying power of the Ankole monarchy lies in the emergence of sub-cleavages among the Bairu. European proselytisation in Ankole had tended to divide the population into roughly equal proportions of Catholics and Protestants. Converted Bahima are almost exclusively Protestants, while Catholic Bairu are in slightly larger numbers than Protestant Bairu. In time, different patterns of socialisation and different economic opportunities have tended to make the Protestant Bairu more antagonistic to the Bahima establishment than were the Catholic Bairu.[35] In the late 1950s, the Catholic Bairu aligned themselves with the Bahima against the Protestant Bairu in the Ankole branch of the Democratic Party, although many Catholic Bairu insist on pointing out that this was done less out of a predilection for traditional authority than for reasons of political expediency. The Catholic Bairu - Bahima alignment involved an implicit understanding, however, that the position of the monarchy would remain unquestioned. Meanwhile, the Protestant Bairu found their way into the Uganda People's Congress and in the early 1960s faced a need to attract votes from either Catholic Bairu or Bahima to stand a chance of winning elections.

As a result, while the UPC membership would have been the most likely group openly to challenge the kingship, electoral considerations caused them to refrain from doing so. Ironically, the two political parties were indeed so concerned not to be identified publicly with anti-monarchical opinion that at times each of them purported to represent the interests of the most loyal defenders of the Omugabe. Little of this stemmed from genuine sympathy for the kingship; but it helped to prolong the relatively undisturbed existence of the monarchy.

Ethnic tension was at its height in Ankole in the middle and late 1950s. However, this was also the time when important advances towards ethnic equality were made, stimulated by political as well as educational and economic conditions.[36] By the time of independence, in 1962, remnants of inequality were certainly still present in Ankole, but the principle of Bahima supremacy was no longer operative and, in many spheres of life, Bairu could be found who stood on an equal footing with Bahima. The friction between Bairu and Bahima slowly subsided, and Bairu protest declined correspondingly. A core of Bairu militants continued to press for full equality, however. Among other things, they did not envisage the possibility of full political emancipation short of a formal abolition of kingship. Its elimination, as it turned out, came at a time when equality in an ethnic sense had by and large been achieved.

Notes

1   See Chapter 2, The apparent paradox and The limits of the power of Nkore kingship.
2   Native Administration, 4.
3   He was not told then, however, that he was 'king'. Roscoe wrote in his preface : 'I have found it advisable in this case to retain the native title of Mugabe for the king in deference to the wishes of the officers at work in the country, who dislike the title of king being used for rulers of small African states'. Roscoe, *op.cit.*, v.

4   With one exception, i.e. Buhweju county, the provision in the Ankole Agreement that the principal chiefs were entitled to nominate their successors had soon fallen into oblivion. But after the erosion of the Bahinda elite a co-optative element was nonetheless retained and the
Bahima establishment had a considerable influence on the appointments that were made.
5   Cf. Fallers, *op.cit., passim.*
6   A note in the margin of the minutes of the meeting of saza chiefs held on 19 May 1938.
7   Letter from the sub-commissioner, Western province, to the chief secretary, Uganda protectorate, on the 20 March 1907. It may be noted that Kahaya was indeed ostensibly treated as a schoolboy, by administrative officers, missionaries and other Europeans alike. Some of this transpires in the following comment: 'As for the King, he has almost to be kept away from the house by main force. I almost think he would like to take up his permanent abode down here. Twice a day he likes to come down, and will not take the broadest hint to go. He is exactly as a child, and one must of necessity act accordingly, and tell him when to go, and make him to do it. But there is no question about his friendliness, only it is not conducive to much work.' *Willis Journal*, II, 328.

The exchange of courtesies with the Omugabe corresponded with these attitudes. It also was somewhat incongruous : '[There arrived some] young heifers from the King, one for each of us. When you think that the price of a cow, sold by government is 50 rupees, and that there is a proverb "What does not kill the Muhima Will not separate him from his cow"', so keen are the Bahima on their cows, this means a good present. Mbaguta, not to be outdone, sent down a fine cow and a calf for Savile and the following morning sent me a beautiful cow, both these last being of the hornless kind, which they say are the best of all. Finally, he sent us down a really magnificent ram. We did not know really what to give in return as our needs are so very different from theirs, and what is useful to us is no good at all to them. However, they are very keen on European boxes: so we got two wooden boxes, painted them red, wrote KAHAYA and MBAGUTA respectively on them, and sent them up. We also gave each a bottle of Eau de Cologne.' *Willis Journal*, 11, 252.
8   Letter from the sub-commissioner, Western province, to the acting collector, Mbarara Collectorate, 20 March 1907.
9   Letter from the acting collector, Mbarara Collectorate, to the sub-commissioner, Western province, 5 March 1907.
10 Letter from the district commissioner, Ankole, to E. S. Kahaya, Omugabe, 17 September 1921.
11 Letter from the provincial commissioner, Western province, to the Omugabe of Ankole, 27 October 1927.
12 Report of the district commissioner, Ankole, on his visit to the Omugabe, 17 March 1933.
13 Letter from the district commissioner, Ankole, to E. S. Kahaya, M.B.E., Omugabe w'Ankole, 10 December 1933.
14 Letter from the provincial commissioner, Western province, to Omugabe of Ankole, 1 February 1926.
15 Letter from provincial commissioner, Western province, to officer-in-charge, Mbarara, 11 April 1927.
16 'Katikiro' and 'Sekibobo' were the Enganzi and the county chief of Mitooma respectively. (The Kiganda term Katikiro was dropped in the 1930s in favour of 'Enganzi'.) Despite the district commissioner's concern, the provincial commissioner decided the matter was a domestic affair of the Omugabe.
17 Letter from the Omugabe to the district commissioner, Ankole, 7 November 1927.
18 Precis of the Omugabe's speech to the Bahima at Nyabushozi, 15 February 1940.
19 Letter from the Omugabe to the district commissioner, Ankole, 29 January 1940.
20 Letter from the Omugabe to the governor of Uganda, 24 November 1944.
21 The meaning of S.A.A.F. is not clear from the record. Possibly it refers to the South African Air Force.

The Redefinition of Kingship 61

22 See the respective district reports for those years.
23 Cook, *Uganda Memories*, 118. Willis' first encounter with Kahaya induced him to adopt somewhat similar notions: 'The King is a young fellow, very much like a great overgrown boy, well over six feet in height and big in every way: huge long flabby hands and enormous slabs of feet – a terrible and significant warning against drinking much milk! *Willis Journal*, I,109. An early anthropological explorer, Cunningham, even took the liberty to take the measurements of Kahaya, which he recorded as follows:

Height, standing in thin sandals	6ft. +	$6\frac{1}{2}$ inch
Chest, under coat		$4\frac{1}{2}$
Neck	1	$4\frac{1}{2}$
Wrist	0	8
Wait, outside garments	5	$7\frac{1}{2}$
Ankle (just above)	1	$7\frac{1}{2}$
Foot (length at)	1	$1\frac{1}{2}$
Weight	301 Ib., or $21\frac{1}{2}$ stone.	

Cunningham commented that 'It will be seen from the measurements that, literally, the King of Ankole is a powerful man. He is just twenty years of age, weighs 301 Ib. And stands 6ft. $6\frac{1}{2}$ inch in height. He is erect, but, as might be expected, not very active. When he travels, he is carried in a large basket slung on poles by a team of the strongest men amongst his following. The team is grouped in fours, and each four carriers take the poles in turn, resting them on their shoulders. On a good road they can travel at a rate of four or five miles an hour.' I. F. Cunningham, *op.cit.*, 20-21.
24 As if to confirm this, paragraph 182 of the Ankole District Annual Report, 1935, states: 'While it cannot be said that [the Omugabe] has given any constructive assistance during the year, it must, on the other hand, be admitted that he has not been the cause of creating any insurmountable difficulties.'
25 Native Administration, 4.
26 E.g. 'a change in any one part of the culture will be accompanied by changes in other parts, and...only by relating any planned detail of change to the central values of the culture is it possible to provide for the repercussions which will occur in other aspects of life.' Margaret Mead, *Cultural Patterns and Technical Change* (Paris, 1953): 10
27 The difficulty was in part terminological. The word 'Bairu' has been used to designate (a) cultivators (b) servants or serfs, and (c) an ethnic category. But only relatively few individuals from the ethnic and cultivating community called 'Bairu' appear to have stood in any direct servant relationship to Bahima lords. Thus, the simple but key fact that one word, 'Bairu', was used to refer at once to a small category of servants, and to the larger population of cultivators unwittingly may have extended the connotation of subordinate status to the larger group, at least 'in the mind of early European travellers and colonial officials. E.g. 'The word "Bairo" is apparently the Hima designation of those whom the proud Hamitic invaders regard as their slaves.' Sir Harry Johnston, *The Uganda Protectorate*. Vol. II, 607.

In Somalia, a similar ambiguity in a not altogether dissimilar situation, namely in regard to the agriculturalist population between the Juba and Shebelle rivers on the one hand and a small group of bondsmen traditionally attached to the pastoralists on the other, caused Lewis to typographically distinguish between Sab for the former and sab for the latter. (1. M. Lewis, *A Pastoral Democracy*, London, 1961:14.)

28 The distinction was the one developed in M. Fortes and E. E. Evans, Pritchard (eds.), *African Political Systems*, London, 1940.

29 Johnston, *op.cit.*, 630. There was one exception to this tendency, although the view concerned was as manifestly unfounded as the praise bestowed upon the Bahima. Before coming to Ankole, Willis reflected 'What one hears of the natives, who are Bahima by race (sic), is not to their credit: they seem to be an idle and untrustworthy people; one hears the same report from all sources. So we shall need much prayer.' *Willis Journal*, I, 101.

30 In the 1930s these powers were virtually institutionalised. A frequent entry under 'Reasons for selection' on forms then used in connection with the appointment and dismissal of chiefs read 'Recommended by Omugabe and his advisers'. Those recommendations were discussed and formulated in meetings of the county chiefs and the Omugabe, in which Mbaguta played a key role.

31 For instance, the Bairu were obliged to perform labour duties, pay tax and provide food supplies for extractive agents who were largely Bahima chiefs, and who themselves enjoyed a substantial share of this revenue. The 'mailo' land grants given to senior Bahima chiefs brought thousands of Bairu directly in a tenant-landlord dependency relationship. The preference in the recruitment of senior chiefs itself continued to be given to Bahima and other non-Bairu almost until the middle of the century.

32 The development of ethnic conflict in Ankole is traced in greater detail in my chapter 'Kumanyana and Rwenzururu: Two Responses to Ethnic Inequality', in Robert I. Rotberg and Ali A. Mazrui, (eds.), *Protest and Power in Black Africa*, New York, 1970.

33 For instance, after a visit to Rwanda, the Omugabe stressed the unity he expected of the Banyankore, in the following terms: 'In Ruanda, there are three types of people, namely Bahutu, Batutsi and the Batwa. They work together in co-operation and...their motto is "Omuguha gw'enyabushuu" (a rope with three strands) representing these classes of people in Ruanda. You will agree with me that no country should expect progress if there is lack of co-operation and disunity. Division and hatred engineered by subversive elements in a country exhibit a gloomy picture and their ends are fatal. I should like you to be "Omuguha gw'enyabushatu". That is when we shall achieve Ankole's will as a nation.' From the speech by Rubambansi the Omugabe at the Opening Ceremony of the Eishengyero of Ankole 17 January 1956.

34 Some further differences are suggested in my article, 'Protest Movements in Western Uganda: Some Parallels and Contrasts', *Kroniek van Africa*, 1970, 3.

35 See my 'Kumanyana and Rwenzururu'.

36 *Ibid.*

5
The Neo-Traditionalisation of Ankole Kingship

A centrally placed institution which has lost its essential purpose cannot just fall into oblivion or wither away. Similar to the dilapidated roof of a house, the collapse might be obstructed by the remaining walls and beams. But as an alternative to oblivion, an institution may be exalted into higher spheres and be made not a ruin but a monument. Either solution implies a removal from the functioning core of the system. Thus, if a political institution is decorated with gilt and glitter, it is conceivable that its functions are subject to decay. And when most references to an institution begin to concern its pomp and circumstance, it is reasonable to suspect that the one-time essence of its role may have ceased to exist. Judging from the Ankole district records, these tendencies appear to have been quite manifest during the last decades of the Obugabeship. From the mid-1930s, in effect, attention was increasingly focused on the ceremonial aspects of kingship, as a result of which the Ankole monarchy became quite lavishly adorned.

The dressing-up was in symbolic as well as in more literal fashion. There was, for example, the question of the state chair. This matter was first raised in 1934, when the district commissioner of Ankole called his superiors' attention to the fact that the Omugabe did not have a throne. He suggested that the governor of Uganda might wish to show his appreciation of the interest then being taken by the Omugabe in the affairs of Ankole through the presentation of a state chair.[1] The governor, however, still considered this too rash an action. As the chief secretary communicated to the provincial commissioner:

> The Governor has learned with great satisfaction that the Mugabe is now showing greater interest in public affairs and the Mugabe may be informed to this effect if you so desire. His Excellency considers, however, that the question of conferring further distinction on the Mugabe should be postponed for a year, by which time it should be possible to find an opinion as to whether the present improvement is likely to be lasting.[2]

As it turned out, the opinion formed after this trial period did not seem to warrant the early conferment of a throne. And in fact, it would take as much as ten years before any further steps were taken concerning this matter. It was then that the Enganzi approached the district commissioner, requesting whether 'the Protectorate Government would kindly provide a Coronation Chair'.[3]

The new district commissioner appeared somewhat at a loss with this request. The Omugabe's demeanour was not so much the problem now. But as he knew a throne to be a very integral part of the emblems of royalty, the district commissioner wondered: 'Are there any symbolic decorations which you want to incorporate in the chair. Please let me know soon'.[4] The reply he got was not without interest for an understanding of the sources of royal symbolism in Ankole. The Enganzi, while forwarding a sketch of Bagyendanwa, the royal drum, submitted: 'As you know this better than I do, I request you to incorporate some decoration in the chair you may deem suitable.'[5]

This limited exchange of communications by itself was of little significance. Taken alone, it would hardly constitute proof that the Obugabeship was being modelled after European style. But similar searches for symbolism occurred in respect of other royal attributes, which seemed to reaffirm the tendency. In 1944, for instance, the Enganzi requested 'that the Government may grant us a crown for the Omugabe to wear on the Coronation Day'.[6]

Apparently taken a little aback by this question, the district commissioner responded: 'Will you please let me know what was the custom in the past when a new Omugabe was crowned? The Crown is such a symbol of the Omugabeship that I feel it should be locally made'.[7] Again, he was soon put in the picture on the tradition of crowns, although the answer may have been somewhat unexpected. For the district commissioner reported to the provincial commissioner that 'it appears...that in the past the Omugabe never had a crown and it is a new idea that he should wear one on his Coronation Day'.[8] Provided with this information, the provincial commissioner for its part concluded that the request was not really based on tradition. To the district commissioner, he directed:

> The use of the term 'Coronation' is inappropriate and should be avoided; similarly, if possible, the term 'crown' or reference to 'kingship'. The native term for the ceremony, if it can be distinguished from the Accession ceremony – and also for the head-dress – should be invariably used. ... I agree that if it is considered by the Banyankore that the Mugabe should wear a special head-dress on ceremonial occasions, one should be made locally. Similar head-dresses in Bunyoro are made mainly of cowrie shells; that of the Mukama of Toro was made for him by his Mother, chiefly of parrot's feathers'.[9]

Now, the provincial commissioner had correctly surmised that a coronation and all it would involve was a novelty for Ankole. As Morris points out, 'the word *engure* (which is really a headband) is borrowed from Luganda and the idea of a 'coronation' is a European importation'.[10] But it seems possible that the provincial commissioner's resistance to the use of terms, such as 'crown', 'coronation' and 'kingship', was not merely for their lack of traditional referents, but was primarily based on a premise that too much exaltation was to be avoided. Judging from the tone of the instruction, there seemed a fear that a too explicit recognition of 'royalty' might elicit identifications and sentiment which could prove harmful to regular administration. If and in as far as that fear existed, it would appear to have been overly pessimistic. Interest in and demands for neo-traditionalisation came indeed, and continued to come, from local quarters. But these were largely restricted to members of the Bahima establishment who, not least because of the vantage point they held in the administration, were in a position to note what standards developed elsewhere in the country. Royal *bon ton* in Uganda in fact largely evolved on such a comparative basis, and neither tradition nor popular opinions in a district like Ankole did necessarily have much to do with it.

However, the determination to oppose anything but 'genuine' tradition did not persist. Before long the door was opened for symbolic innovations of many kinds, virtually inaugurating *regalia galore*. A full-fledged coronation ceremony, for example, was held in 1945 on the occasion of the accession of Omugabe Gasyonga, some of the colour of which was indicated by the enlistment of the services of Mr Georgiadis in Alexandria. Georgiadis was asked to provide a suitable 'Ceremonial Robe embroidered in gilded silver threads' for the Omugabe.[11] Also, one of the high moments in the ceremonies was the 'crowning' of the Omugabe, performed by Bishop Stuart of Uganda. Several years later, in 1964, a resolution was submitted that the place where the Omugabe was crowned should be 'preserved and kept as a monument to remember the day in future'. The argument then was that the kingdoms of Buganda and Toro had 'examples of such places of royal significance'. Moreover, it was argued, 'such places could boost tourist trade'.[12]

In later years, the anniversary of the Omugabe's accession became an important annual event in Ankole. For these celebrations, the Enganzi at one time provided a rationalisation in the following terms:

> In the past years, the birthday or accession ceremonies of our late Omugabe, like those of his contemporaries, were not observed as it was impossible to know their exact dates. With the new generation, however, it has been possible to know the dates of these events and consequently in Buganda, Bunyoro and Toro these ceremonies are held every year by new rulers who succeeded their predecessors. Our new Omugabe has just succeeded to the Ankole throne and so it is our great desire that he should not be the exception.[13]

Thus, each year on 26 September, elaborate festivities were staged in Mbarara to celebrate the Omugabe's coronation anniversary. They had little to do with Ankole tradition, but they served to suggest status and dignity through the display of pomp and protocol which was their characteristic feature. The programme for these occasions ran from church services to sundowners and included standard items such as a march past by school children, the inspection of a guard of honour (not mounted by any Ankole constabulary but by the Uganda Police), the release of prisoners, speech-making and football matches. Not least of interest was the detailed care which went into establishing the order of precedence in which visiting dignitaries would take part in the proceedings.[14]

The tendency to make Ankole royalty more royal also entailed the redesignation of many contingent elements in the system. Early on, already, various quasi-traditional chiefly titles had been introduced under the auspices of Ankole's monarchical status. Among the titles which had thus gained currency were those of the county or saza chiefs, and of senior officials: *Omuramuzi* (chief judge), *Omubiki* (treasurer), *Kihimba* (administrative secretary), and *Omujasi* (head of Ankole askaris). Most of these styles happened to be borrowed, again, from Buganda, but while proposals were raised from time to time to 'ankole-ize' them, it turned out that Ankole tradition offered insufficient equivalents to make this operational: [15]

Styles were also reconsidered for the circles most intimately associated with the Omugabe. Western models for royal family patterns seemed reflected in questions concerning the proper nomenclature for the Omugabe's official wife and children. In the past, Roscoe asserted, 'it was quite evident that there never was a queen'.[16] In 1945, however, the *Eishengyero* (district council) debated whether the Omugabe's wife should be called *Omwigarire* or just Omugabe's wife, and a conclusion was reached in favour of the former term.[17] The English equivalent was accepted to be Queen. Again, the Omugabe's children became known as princes and princesses, and the family's composition thus came to resemble that of a standard royal house.

Inevitably, perhaps, other questions also arose about proper royal standing. Their significance lay not so much in their contents or in the way they were resolved, but rather in the fact that they were raised at all. A few examples may illustrate this point. In 1952, the Eishengyero was asked to discuss the desirability of acquiring a 'special dress' for the Omwigarire, which did not prove difficult to decide. As one member submitted, 'she had a good dress which she had put on at Coronation Day and that could serve', which was an argument with which the council concurred.[18] A year later, similar questions were raised, and similarly resolved, in respect to the Omugabe's children. Again, the Eishengyero did not see grounds to assume responsibility for their style of dress on public occasions.[19] Meanwhile, however, considerable care was given to a rather different matter, the memory of kings for which the Ankole government agreed to build a mausoleum.

There were still other ways in which the monarchy was dressed up. Most of these again were trivial matters but together they created a pattern and image. The Omugabe's residence, for instance, came to be known as *Mugaba* (palace), as distinguished from the more humble traditional term *ekyikari* (enclosure). A sizeable two-storey building, the palace showed but little regal inspiration, traditional or modern, in its interior decoration. Also, a Royal Standard was designed for the Omugabe, 'set on yellow cloth with his Coat of Arms, drums in white and a lion in brown, against a black background'.[20] In 1954, the words *Omugabe-Ishe-Nyina-Bagyendanwa* (Omugabe-Father-Mother-Bagyendanwa) were inserted into all official stamps and seals of the Ankole government.[21] And in 1959 the picture of the Omugabe and Bagyendanwa were to appear on opposite sides of a medal, to be awarded to individuals who had distinguished themselves in his service.[22] Again, there was the Eishengyero's resolution to display the Omugabe's photograph in all official buildings in Ankole, and its subsequent ruling, as of 1956, that the picture of the Omwigarire should also be shown in the Eishengyero Hall.[23] In the same year also, there was some concern that the Omugabe's platform in the Eishengyero Hall was not of adequate beauty and standard. A decision was reached in favour of such improvements as would 'show both tribal and Western fashions'.[24] Clearly, the pursuit of regalia led in many directions.

Only in a few cases did the search for decorum involve an attempt to preserve or to revive traditional cultural attributes. One such example concerned the customary greeting due to the Omugabe; in the district records it was more than once reaffirmed that this should be given in the traditionally proper way: *Osingyire Nyakusinga*, and *Obukama Nyakusinga* for bidding farewell.[25] The motive for reiterating these forms, as stated, was that they were falling into disregard.

The best example of successful preservation, however, remained Bagyendanwa, the royal drum. This was kept in a specially built house, which was maintained out of Ankole government sources. The drum had a permanent keeper, an old lady of the Bakururu clan, among whose duties was to ensure that the fire burning for it would never go out. A striking degree of personification was strenuously maintained in respect to Bagyendanwa: the drum had its own land and herd of cattle, and was referred to as an individual, Bagyendanwa was flanked to the right by his 'wife' and to the left by his 'enganzi'. Nonetheless, no matter how admirably it was done, this preservation essentially amounted to the upkeep of an antiquity. Apart from the keeper of Bagyendanwa, virtually nobody in Ankole believed that the drum's disappearance would really cause the end of the world. Irreverently, radical Bairu regarded the whole thing as no more than a piece of wood.

Indicatively, perhaps, not a few traditional attributes of the kingship appeared in decline at the very time that new royal decoration was being introduced. This tendency was of no mean importance for the monarchical image in Ankole. The moon ceremonies, for instance, traditionally a central ingredient of the royal culture, in recent decades fell wholly into disregard. Reputedly, the reason was that the knowledge of the special drum-beat, which was a requisite for this festive ritual, had been lost. But perhaps this argument was only another way of conveying that the conditions and interests at the Omugabe's court offered little encouragement for these skins to be handed over. A similar decline occurred in respect to the royal music of Ankole.[26] Originally involving three bands of sixty musicians each, they were first reduced to thirty, later to eleven musicians per band. Moreover, while traditionally these musicians had formed part of the Omugabe's immediate retinue, in recent times they lived in various parts of Ankole and performed in Mbarara only a few times a year – commonly complaining about their low pay. More indicative even of the decline of this music, as in the case of the moon ceremonies, was that a good many of the songs and tunes which once comprised the heritage of Ankole's royal music became irretrievably lost during the present century.

In some of these respects, the Ankole monarchy was quite different from the monarchies in Toro and Bunyoro (not to speak of Buganda). In these other two kingdoms, comparable ingredients of traditional royal culture were kept alive until the last moment of royalty and had also succeeded in coexisting with modern elements. Perhaps this difference from the Ankole case was explicable in terms of the greater degree of popular support commanded by the Toro and Bunyoro monarchies, due, it seems, to their more homogeneous core populations. In Ankole, the social situation which provided the environment and cultural basis of court life was quite thin, even more so since the majority of Bahima were continuously on the move and not in immediate contact with the Omugabe. There was, in fact, only one small group which had acted as a cultural support to the kingship in recent times, namely the Bahima-led *Abataremwa ba Rubambansi* ('Those who never fail Rumbambansi'). For some time around 1962, this circle staged semi-traditional poetry recitations in honour of the Omugabe, though after a number of such meetings nothing more was heard of it.

Somewhat sadly, the loss of royal glamour in Ankole was not only apparent in respect to traditional features, but even with some of the novel ornamentations of kingship. In and around Mbarara, a number of signboards in public places which had been named after the Omugabe were found removed one after the other; one of them that of 'Omugabe's Dam' whose disappearance was noted on the eve of the 1965 accession celebrations. These tendencies accentuated the fact that, apart from an incidental group such as the *Abateremwa*, the monarchy had come to depend almost exclusively on the formal government structure for its survival and sustenance.

The eclipse of the monarchy

The kingship thus increasingly came to be a lonely station. So far from being the axis from which radiated an innovating tradition, in its terminal years the monarchy did little more than reflect the orientations of its environment. And the shine it produced was just as faint as the popular identifications which it inspired.

A lonely monarch, the Omugabe's loneliness was made even more apparent by the pedestal on which he was placed during the last phase of his reign. Whereas in earlier colonial times his status had been deliberately downgraded in the interest of administrative efficiency, throughout the fifties and the early sixties the tendency was just the opposite. Not only was he knighted, but in these later years formal recognition was given to some of the Omugabe's traditional titles. In 1951, the provincial commissioner gave his approval to the use of the title of 'Rubambansi the Omugabe' 'on all formal occasions as a matter of courtesy'.[27] Similarly, when discussing the proposals for local government reform outlined in the 1953 Wallis report, members of the Eishengyero suggested that the Omugabe be treated as the political head of the kingdom 'as he had always been'.[28] It was further decided in that same year that from now on all by-laws would be ratified by the Omugabe before being published in the *Gazette* and should read 'The Omugabe has given his consent to...'[29] Moreover, as if to reaffirm his newly-gained pre-eminence, the Omugabe was allowed to officiate over the annual opening ceremonies of the Eishengyero and to award Certificates of Honour to those Ankole government employees deemed worthy of such distinction.'[30] Lastly, it was submitted in this new climate that the Omugabe should be accompanied on his official tours by 'one or two senior officials in their cars' since 'going alone would be risky to his life and would belittle his dignity.[31]

Many of these innovations might have been thought of as part of the normal routine of a constitutional monarch. In Ankole, however, the political context and the background of social divisions and transformations in the district turned out not to be very conducive to their assimilation. Instead, the varying fortunes in the district political arena continued to add strength to these 'constraints'. Up until the mid-fifties the Eishengyero had remained largely a Bahima establishment. After 1955, however, following franchise extensions, its composition underwent a major change; from then on until about 1961, the position of the Bahima elite suffered a sharp decline. This transformation was reflected in the Eishengyero's increasingly cavalier treatment of certain proposals aiming at butstressing the symbolic aspects of the Obugabeship, such as the defeat of a motion introduced in 1957 seeking the confirmation of all appointed chiefs by the Omugabe.[32] Only in a new political constellation, in 1964, could this idea be reintroduced. From then on, in fact, new chiefs were expected to thank the Omugabe for their appointment and pledge loyalty to him on Accession Day; but as it transpired, some of the chiefs never turned up on these occasions.

Thus, the loss of effective powers by the Omugabe continued to be paralleled by attempts to enhance the formal appurtenances of his office. As an Eishengyero motion of 1961 stated it, the 'Omugabe was to be the Head of all people in Ankole except for Her Majesty the Queen and her representative, the Governor of Uganda'.[33] But this declaration itself only appeared to increase the imbalance between the lofty and low standings accorded from different perspectives to Ankole kingship.

The inflation of the Obugabeship reached its peak shortly after Uganda attained independence. The stature and dignity of the office of Omugabe gained unprecedented recognition – a phenomenon which is best understood in the light of two fundamental realities of post-independence Uganda politics. One was the adoption of a special kind of federal structure for the new state; another had to do with the somewhat capricious course of party competition in the years immediately following independence.

'Federalism' explicitly put Ankole on the political map of Uganda as a kingdom. As noted earlier, there was a variety of reasons for adopting a pluralistic constitutional framework for Uganda, the most decisive being the position of Buganda. In contrast with Ankole, the kingdom of Buganda had formed a powerful political sub-system, whose integration within the rest of Uganda posed serious problems first to colonial officials and subsequently to national Ugandan politicians. For a long time, both felt that Buganda could not be dethroned from its dominant position without seriously compromising the viability of Uganda as a whole.[34] Until the mid-sixties the solution adopted to contend with the Buganda issue was to try to balance its influence by enhancing that of the smaller kingdoms, and even of the districts of Uganda, which hence were all turned into minor replicas of Buganda. In so far as possible, the traditional and quasi-traditional rulers of these divisions were placed on an equal constitutional footing with the Kabaka of Buganda and this effort contributed in no small part to the exaltation of offices such as that of the Omugabe of Ankole.

The constitutional framework in which these arrangements were worked out at independence was federal in respect to Buganda, and semi-federal or quasi-federal in respect to Ankole, Toro, Bunyoro, and the 'territory' of Busoga. Until this pattern was laid down, the term 'kingdom' had been used in an informal sense in respect to Ankole and the other semi-traditional units. The common official reference being 'district'. Only shortly before independence, the 'Kingdom of Ankole' and the other western Uganda kingdoms had gained constitutional recognition *qua* kingdoms.

Ankole's monarchical status was formalised in a new Ankole Agreement, concluded on 30 August 1962, and was reaffirmed in the 1962 independence constitution of Uganda as well as in subsequent legislation. The wording used for defining the position of the Omugabe was the same in the Ankole Agreement and the Uganda constitution: [35]

> (1) The Omugabe (King), who is the Ruler of Ankole, shall enjoy all the titles, dignities, and pre-eminence that attach to the office of Omugabe under the law and custom of Ankole. (2) The Omugabe, the Omwigarire (Queen) and members of the Royal Family, that is to say, descendants of Omugabe Rwebishengye (Abanyiginya n'Abanyiginyakazi), shall enjoy their customary titles and precedence.

The signing of the 1962 Ankole Agreement was hailed as the 'biggest ceremony in Ankole history'[36], and for several dignitaries it was indeed an opportune moment to look back into the past. The bishop of Mbarara outlined three stages in the development of Ankole – 'the period when the Kings of Ankole were supreme, their period under British protection, and the time after the agreement had been signed by the Governor and the Omugabe'.[37] The Enganzi, for his part, pointed to the changes which had occurred since 1901 and asked 'those present to join with him in asking the Governor to convey to the Queen (of England) and her Government the deep gratitude of the people of Ankole' for the work they had done.[38] The Omugabe, the Enganzi, and the governor all expressed satisfaction with the constitutional arrangements which had just been agreed upon.[39]

While the new Ankole Agreement thus substantially enhanced the formal status of the Omugabe, this trend was curiously accentuated by the local implications of party rivalries at the national level. It should be remembered that at the time of independence, in 1962, the central government of Uganda was under the control of a coalition between the Uganda People's Congress (UPC) and Kabaka Yekka (KY), while the Ankole government was under control of the Democratic Party (DP). By 1963, however, the UPC had evicted the DP from its leading position in Ankole, and before 1964 drew to a close a growing tension emerged between the UPC and KY, in time causing the collapse of their alliance at the centre. Exclusive control over the central government passed into the hands of the UPC leadership; meanwhile the tension between the UPC and KY reached unprecedented proportions.

In 1962, Kabaka Yekka (The Kabaka Only) began to solicit the support of Baganda and non-Baganda elements residing in Ankole. In response to what was officially regarded in Ankole as an unwarranted intrusion into the political life of the kingdom, the DP government of Ankole initiated measures to counteract the KY tactics. Thus, when groups of individuals in Ankole began to wear badges bearing the words 'Kabaka Yekka', the Ankole government reacted by prohibiting the display of such badges on the ground that it amounted to 'praising a King in another Kingdom, and this was contrary to customary law as it belittled the honour and authority of the Omugabe',[40] One Muhamudu Kasumba was arrested and convicted for not heeding the Ankole government's instructions, and a case grew out of the incident in which the action of the Ankole government was finally upheld as valid by the Uganda High Court.[41]

The matter became rather more complicated because some members of the Uganda cabinet did not, at that time, share the view that wearing a KY badge constituted an affront to the Omugabe. At a political rally in Mbarara in July, 1962, some central government ministers went so far as to publicly denounce the order which sought to prevent the wearing of KY badges. The minister of justice, himself a Munyankore and UPC member, 'shouted praises of Kabaka Yekka and told a big gathering that anyone was free to wear a Kabaka Yekka badge in Ankole'.[42] These controversies led to a growing estrangement between the Ankole and Uganda governments, and similarly between the minister of justice and the High Court.

The issue took a new turn when those who sought to spread KY influence in Ankole adopted an alternative strategy. With characteristic shrewdness, they substituted another label for the previous one and soon new badges were circulating bearing the inscription *Omugabe Wenka* (Omugabe Only).

The display of these badges was immediately prohibited, however, and *Omugabe Wenka* turned out to be an exceedingly shortlived affair. But it seems a fair presumption that even without the government's prohibition its impact would have remained minimal. Neither the persons wearing these badges nor the slogan itself carried much of an appeal in Ankole. The comments of the Omugabe sought to defuse the issue: [43]

> I am above politics and the use of my name by any one political party as a slogan would only divide my people and endanger their happiness and the progress of my Kingdom ...I do not discriminate against any of my people and I regard all of them in Ankole, irrespective of their political or religious beliefs, as my beloved subjects and for that reason I do not permit a section of my people to use my name for political ends.

And in regard to Kabaka Yekka, the Omugabe's view was :

> My Enganzi and the Eishengyero have publicly condemned Kabaka Yekka activities in Ankole and I strongly endorse their condemnations as I would not personally permit any other ruler to exercise his rule in my own Kingdom.

The KY threat against the Omugabe's kingdom was repeated a few years later, but now in an entirely different political context. Ironically, the renewed Kabaka Yekka infiltration caused the UPC government then in office in Ankole to use much the same argument as its DP predecessor had done. On 14 September 1965, the Enganzi stated 'I have today been informed that a movement called Kabaka Yekka has started infiltrating into this Kingdom to try and hinder the progress of this Kingdom.' He further pointed out that 'saying Kabaka Yekka here in Ankole and wearing Kabaka Yekka shirts in Ankole means that the Kabaka is the only King...even in this Kingdom of Ankole', and warned that 'I, as the guardian of the constitution under the Ankole schedule and the Omugabe's Government as a whole cannot approve of this.'[44] To the Omugabe the Enganzi gave his reassurance that 'this Government and your loyal subjects shall never allow any external movement seeking to lower your dignity.

'The exodus of KY to this kingdom is truly calculated at lowering your dignity and seeks to cause division among your loyal subjects. Banyankore are wellknown to be peace-loving and tolerant. But they might be forced to reach a point beyond which they will tolerate no more if KY tries to force its way through to this Kingdom.'[45]

That point was never reached, however, partly because of the restrictions placed upon KY activities, and partly because far more critical developments were in the offing. From the end of 1965 until mid-1966, Uganda experienced one of the most acute crises of its history as an independent state, and through the spring of 1966 everyone's attention was focused on the impending trial of strength between the kingdom of Buganda and the central government of Uganda. The outcome of the crisis was to bring about a major change in the national balance of power and in time produced a considerable overhaul of the entire governmental structure.

It was also this crisis which provided the immediate motive for abolishing monarchical structures throughout Uganda. Significantly, just like the earlier policies which had so much contributed to the exaltation of the western Uganda kingdoms, the measure again stemmed basically from a strategy pursued in regard to Buganda. When the Buganda crisis came to a head, the Uganda government seized upon this opportunity to dismantle once and for all the Kabaka's stronghold. Following an open clash with the armed forces of Uganda, the Buganda monarchy was destroyed and its Kabaka fled the country. With the Buganda kingship eliminated, the smaller kingdoms instantly lost their raison d' etre from the standpoint of the Uganda government; moreover, their abolition was positively valued because it 'coated the pill', as it were, for Buganda.

From the perspective of Uganda-wide politics, therefore, this whole series of events provided a major illustration of the part played by national political considerations – and more specifically by the strategies employed in an internal balance of power situation – first in retaining and ultimately in abolishing the

Ankole monarchy: whether or not the Ankole kingship enjoyed legitimacy within its own society was of secondary importance in either period.

The Ankole monarchy's last year of existence provided final confirmation of its status as a dependent variable. Following the 1966 clash, the preparation of new constitutional arrangements took some time, and while new proposals were being formulated many pre-existing arrangements and institutions were temporarily left untouched. Among these were the kingships of Ankole, Toro and Bunyoro. In 1966, an interim constitution was introduced which for all intents and purposes abolished federalism, but nonetheless reconfirmed the existence of these three remaining monarchies. As the Enganzi then said to the Omugabe, in his opening address of the Eishengyero, 'nothing in this constitution has prejudiced your position as the Omugabe of Ankole Kingdom, as you will soon hear ...Part one paragraph one to ten of the Ankole New Schedule, which honours you Nyakusinga, has not been altered either by letter or punctuation'.[46] But the provisional 1966 constitution was in effect for a little over a year, that is, until new constitutional arrangements for a unitary republic in Uganda were ready. The Ankole kingship lasted until just that time.

Symbolic exaltation and institutional relevance or decline: four configurations[47]

It will be clear from the foregoing chapters that, as an institution, the Ankole kingship during the twentieth century was subject to neo-traditionalisation as well as to institutional decay. Still, this may leave unexplored more specific questions concerned with the ways in which patterns of neo-traditionalisation, as manifested in increasing ceremonialisation or other forms of symbolic exaltation, may relate to issues of institutional relevance and decline. Under what conditions would it seem justified to point to neo-traditionalisation as a potential index of institutional decline? In other words, to what extent is it possible to generalise about this connection, and what does the Ankole case exemplify in this regard?

The Ankole example seems relatively straightforward and in a sense simpler than many others because the ceremonialisation of its kingship was paralleled by growing popular indifference and, in the end, by quite lukewarm reactions to the monarchy's abolition. Whether symbolic exaltation equals institutional decline and redundancy is another matter, however. Several examples from recent decades raise questions about that; for example, the cases of Emperor Bokassa and of Field Marshal-cum-President Idi Amin. Each of these figures, in his heyday and in his own way, indulged in many novel forms of ceremony and symbolic exaltation, often with an inventiveness and a taste for the grandiose that would have made Ankole's Omugabe seem extremely modest by contrast. Whatever else could be observed about them, they did not exactly appear to be 'in decline' when they were at the centre of things. Or were they? What they had was power, not allegiance; whatever allegiance they might have had was clearly dwindling. This distinction is potentially important and should be explored further.

Meanwhile, there are other possible reservations to the equation of symbolic exaltation and institutional decline. One is derived from the Nkore context, Ankole's direct precursor as a political unit, where as we have seen the Omugabe was invested with some kind of above-average qualities. What is more, it seemed that adherence to the myth of his omnipotence was in some way 'functional' in terms of maintaining the political cohesiveness of the society. In the absence by and large of an administrative apparatus that could enforce collective decisions, this was in fact virtually the only antidote to centrifugal forces. Paradoxically, though, the 'functionality' or 'relevance' of symbolic exaltation for maintaining an institutional context seems to denote rather the reverse of symbolic exaltation as an index of institutional decline. Once again, therefore, there is reason to question whether these opposites can be reconciled.

Some further reservations are implied in a very different form of precedent. Is it not institutionalisation *par excellence,* one might argue, if, in regard to a particular office, careful attention is paid persistently to subtleties of decorum, protocol and public image? If one takes two celebrated examples – those of the Vatican and British royalty until some years ago – it is difficult to see how they could have maintained their special image and position except through continuous and meticulous care of symbols and symbolism – coupled, to be sure, with a good intuitive insight into what the public's eye demands. *Prima facie,* it would seem difficult to argue that these examples represented institutional decline rather than institutionalisation. In recent years that logic has been less self-evident in the case of the British monarchy, though the wide-ranging public discussion and the pledges made to 'modernise' the royal house in the wake of the death of Princess Diana seemed to re-affirm recognition of these crucial linkages.

In sum, therefore, four distinct positions suggest themselves regarding the relationship between manifestations of symbolic exaltation and questions of institutional relevance and decline. The first, exemplified by colonial Ankole, amounts to quasi-traditional ceremonialisation paralleling and, in fact, camouflaging institutional decline and loss of effective power. Second, there are the cases of Bokassa and others, which exhibited grandiose ceremonisalisation combined with the exercise of excessive coercive power. Third, comes the example of pre-colonial Nkore, which seemed to have exaltation as a sort of substitute for central power; and fourth, we have neo-tradionalisation as an index of institutionalisation.

The first and second of these, though at extreme ends from each other, in terms of the central rulers' effective powers, are perhaps less contradictory than they might appear at first sight. In the final analysis, both try to make up for, or cover up, what is essentially the same sort of predicament – namely, an acute lack of popular support and allegiance. These two situations have that in common, notwithstanding the fact that in one the ruler exercises absolute power, while in the other he is absolutely powerless. Together they re-emphasise that form and expression in lieu of substance is an old phenomenon indeed, predating even its baroque versions and certainly constituting the recurrent feature in the contemporary context.

But how does this position relate to the third connection between power and symbolism, that is, the situation where symbolic exaltation almost seems to take the place of central power? Part of the answer must be that this cannot really be a matter of substitutes. Although the precolonial Nkore system lacked a central state apparatus, it nonetheless had a definite collective power basis in the form of the senior chiefs in command of physical forces. In part, it probably was the case that this collective body politic needed to find (symbolic) ways in which to present itself and be recognised. Moreover, the symbolism that had developed around the Omugabe may have functioned internally as a mechanism to ensure stability and as an antidote to mutual rivalry within the collectivity.

Although quite different therefore from the mock symbolism characteristic of the earlier examples, given the quite different structural background, this distinction hardly seems to obviate the need for *a priori* scepticism in regard to manifestations of ceremonial exaltation. Rather, it would seem that the kind of symbolic imagery through which the collective body politic of Nkore sought to assert a common political identity may have been closer to certain examples of 'institutionalised' symbolism, such as that of the Vatican, identified above as the fourth distinct configuration. Notwithstanding their vast differences of scale and elaborateness, and their differentiation of functions, the two latter cases had in common that the incumbents of central roles performed essentially symbolic functions. To followers and outsiders alike, they suggest a supreme level of unity and power associated with these roles although, on closer inspection, this impression may not reflect quite accurately the level and diversity of actual power divisions. In fact, an inverse correlation is again suggested, namely, the greater the ceremonialisation of a particular role, possibly the weaker the actual 'command' powers of its incumbents. Is it not the case, for example, that, like the Omugabe of Nkore, the papal incumbents of the Vatican – with its worldly presence reduced to an absolute minimum – basically have no way to exert power except by calling on certain suprahuman and metaphysical values or qualities? Both the Pope and the

Omugabe, incidently, have been viewed as direct earthly representatives of God and Ruhanga respectively.

But to consider these inverse relationships between symbolism and actual power is by no means to deny that spiritual or ideological influence may emanate from a particular office, role, or institution. In some instances including the two just mentioned, such influence may, in fact, be extremely pervasive and therefore powerful. It is even conceivable that this non-physical (but so highly visible) 'power' will constitute a key antidote to centrifugal forces, ensuring the continued cohesiveness of the political or religious community concerned. That again was found to hold true for the Omugabe of Nkore and has largely been applicable to the Vatican.

The particular kind and quality of influence that may radiate from a symbolic office (however weak it might otherwise be) has evidently caught the attention of many political figures and aspiring leaders who hope to cultivate rapport and obtain support from the populace. It is evident that this symbolic power cannot work unless there is indeed such a sense of popularity, allegiance, and legitimacy to begin with. Examples of its working *do* no doubt occur, though they are definitely fewer than they are claimed to be. In fact, it is quite probably because such examples are known to have occurred and are conceivable in the first place that mock symbolism such as that identified among the first and second types above can occur at all, offering form in lieu of substance. For this reason, too, and especially in the light of its new ceremonial, Ankole kingship seemed to belong to the surrogate, rather than to the genuine, variety.

Thus we have a double inversion: of 'high' symbolism and weak actual powers; and of 'mock' symbolism and lack of popular allegiance. In reality, to be sure, these inverse correlations may well occur in some fused form. In particular, the dividing line between examples of high symbolic exaltation and mock ceremonial is one along which variations and mutations are likely to be found in day-to-day reality. Movement through time is equally conceivable along this line. The Nkore-Ankole case is indeed an example of such movement; increasingly, it has shifted from the first to the second kind of inversion, or, in other words, from an intrinsically symbolic role into its caricature. As it happened, the change remained relatively minor in terms of actual power: at both ends of the line, the Omugabe's powers vis-à-vis the other forces within the political context of Nkore and Ankole, respectively, were quite limited.

Finally, while such distinctions and contrasts may be traced at many levels, in diverse contexts and different historical epochs, thus adding a certain universal quality to the phenomena as analytical problems, it is interesting to note that they were also identified in this way in times long past. Thus, Gibbon, universal quality to the phenomena as analytical problems, it is interesting to note that they were also identified in this way in times long past. Thus, Gibbon, in *The Decline and Fall of the Roman Empire*, contrasted the exaltation and actual powers of the German and Roman emperors, respectively, in a way that is still perfectly relevant to our present concerns: 'If we annihilate the interval of time and space between Augustus and Charles, strong and striking will be the contrast between the two Caesars; the Bohemian, who concealed his weaknesses under the mask of ostentation, and the Roman who disguised his strength under the semblance of modesty' (Gibbon, 1789: 312). Again, *plus ça change, plus c'est la même chose.*

Notes

1. Letter from the provincial commissioner, Western province, to the chief secretary, Uganda protectorate, 20 December 1934.
2. Letter from the chief secretary, Uganda protectorate, to the Provincial commissioner, Western province, 3 January 1935.
3. Letter from the Enganzi to the district commissioner. Ankole, 9 November 1944.
4. Letter from the district commissioner. Ankole, to the Enganzi, 12 January 1945.
5. Letter from the Enganzi to the district commissioner of Ankole, 24 January 1945.
6. Letter from the Enganzi to the District Commissioner, Ankole, 9 November 1944.
7. Letter from the district commissioner, Ankole, to the Enganzi, 18 November 1944.
8. Letter from the district commissioner, Ankole, to the provincial commissioner, Western province, 12 December 1944.
9. Letter from the provincial commissioner, Western province, to the district commissioner, Ankole 18 December 1944.
10. Morris, *The Heroic Recitations*, 82.
11. Letter from acting resident, Buganda, to chief secretary, Uganda protectorate, 9 August 1945.
12. News Release, Department of Information, Uganda government, 11 July. 1964.
13. Letter from Enganzi and chiefs to provincial commissioner, 12 June 1947.
14. For example, the programme for the Omugabe's twentieth Accession Day, 27 September 1965 included :

8.40 a.m.	All distinguished people take their seats at St James Cathedral, Ruharo, for Service.
8.45 a.m.	Constitutional Heads arrive and take their seats.
8.50 a.m.	Prime Minister's arrival at the Church.
8.55 a.m.	Arrival of Ssabasaja Kabaka, the Abakama and the Kyabazinga of Busoga.
9.00 a.m.	Arrival of Rubambansi the Omugabe accompanied by the Enganzi and his Ministers.
9.15 a.m.	Beginning of Church Services at Ruharo, Nyamitanga (R.C.M.) and Nyamitanga Mosque.
10.00 a.m.	Procession from Ruharo to Mugaba Palace: Rubambansi the Omugabe, leading the Procession followed by Ssabasaja Kabaka, Prime Minister, Ag. Chief Justice, Abakama, Kyabazinga of Busoga, the Enganzi, and Ankole Ministers, Central Government Ministers, Constitutional Heads and others.
10.15 a.m.	School children and students March Past at the Palace.
11.30 a.m.	Inspect Guard of Honour mounted by Uganda police. All guests seated in the Eishengyero Hall.
11.40 a.m.	Speeches in the following order: (a) Enganzi's speech (b) Prime Minister's speech

              (c) Omugabe's speech, followed by release of 9 prisoners.
    12.45 a.m.   Refreshments to school children and students.
    1.00 p.m.   Luncheon for invited guests only at Mugaba Palace, and the Rural Training
                 Centre, Kamukuzi.
    2.35 p.m.   Leave palace for Kakyeka stadium.
    2.45 p.m.   Arrive at Kakyeka to watch the following :
    3.00-4.30 p.m. -Uganda Police mounting Parade.
    4.30-5.10 p.m. -Netball
    5.15-6.55 p.m. -Football
    8.00 p.m.   Sundowner for invited guests only at Mugaba Palace.
    10.30 p.m.   The Prime Minister, Dr. A. M. Obote, will open a DANCE at Aga Khan School.
15 What is more, the titles of the county chiefs (Kahima, Kitunzi, Kangaho, Pokino, Kaigo, Mukwenda, Sekibobo, Katambara, Kashwiju and Mugyema) each had a specific meaning in the Buganda context though not in Ankole.
16 Roscoe, *op.cit.*, 34.
17 Minute 13 of the Eishengyero, July 1945.
18 Minute 47 of the Eishengyero, June 1952.
19 Minute 90 of the Eishengyero, 8 July 1953.
20 *Uganda Argus* (Kampala, 16 March 1964).
21 Minute 18 of the Eishengyero, 20 April 1954.
22 Minute 47 of the Eishengyero, 9 October 1959.
23 Minute 42 of the Eishengyero, June 1952, and minutes of the Eishengyero of 17 to 23 January 1956.
24 Minute 27 of the Eishengyero, 1956.
25 Minute 31 of the Eishengyero, 18 October, 1948, and *Report of the Ankole Kingdom Customary Laws' Committee*, Mbarara, 1964
26 Paul van Thiel, 'The Music of the Kingdom of Ankole', *African Music*, IV, I, 6-20.
27 Letter provincial commissioner, Western province, to district commissioner. Ankole, 23 July 1951.
28 Minute 3 of the Eishengyero, May 1953.
29 Minute 46 of the Eishengyero, May 1953.
30 Minute 70 of the Eishengyero 1954.
31 Minute 24 of the Eishengyero, 1957. In recent times, though, the Omugabe was more than once left out from public functions, as some political leaders from Ankole wanted to avoid identification with what they felt was a symbol of Bahima overrule.
32 Minute 25 of the Eishengyero, 1957. The idea was copied from Buganda, where the presentation of chiefs to the Kabaka was known as *Okweyanza*.
33 Minute 67 of the Eishengyero, 1961
34 See David E. Apter, *The Political Kingdom in Uganda: A Study in Bureaucratic Nationalism*, Princeton, 1961
35 See Schedule 2 of the Constitution of Uganda, 1962.
36 *Agetereine*, 14 September 1962.
37 *Uganda Argus*, 31 August 1962.
38 *Ibid.*
39 The Agreement had been worked out in consultation with the governor by a constitutional committee consisting of Ankole representatives. There had only been two points of difference which needed to be referred to the colonial secretary for settlement. One of these was whether or not the Ankole ministers were to enjoy individual or collective responsibility, the other concerned the number of guns to be fired for the Omugabe on ceremonial occasions. On the first issue, the final decision was that they were individually responsible, which meant they

were essentially department heads. On the number of guns 'the committee demanded fifteen while the Governor was only prepared to grant nine', (*Uganda Argus*, 5 March, 1962.) In the end, he got nine.

40 News release, Enganzi of Ankole, undated (August, 1962).
41 Criminal Revision, No.30 of 1962 of the Kashari County Court of Ankole.
42 Open letter from Enganzi to governor of Uganda, 10 August 1962.
43 *Uganda Argus*. 9th February, 1962.
44 'Official Statement by the Enganzi; Warning to K.Y. infiltration in Ankole', 14 September 1965, mimeo.
45 'Speech by Owekitinisa the Enganzi on the 20th Coronation Anniversary of Rubambansi the Omugabe of Ankole, Sir Charles Godfrey Gasyonga 11', 27 September 1965. mimeo.
46 'Speech by Ow'Ekitinisa the Enganzi on the Opening of the First Eishengyero of Ankole', 1 April 1966, mimeo.
47 Originally published as part of Chapter 5 in my book, *Institutionalising Development Policies and Resources Strategies in Eastern Africa and India: Developing Winners and Losers*, Macmillian/Palgrave 2000

Left: *Nuwa Mbaguta – the first Enganzi of Ankole kingdom in the early years of British colonial rule*

Right: *Lazaro Kahaya II – the first Omugabe of colonial Ankole under whom the decline of the Ankole kingship began*

The royal drum (Bagyendanwa), with its consort Kabembura and attendant drums as they used to be kept by their keeper of the Baruru clan
(From H.F. Morris, **A history of Ankole***, Kampala, 1962)*

Left: Sir Charles Godfrey Gasyonga II, the last Omugabe of Ankole kingdom deposed in 1967
Right: James Kahigiriza, the last Enganzi of Ankole and now chairman of Nkore Cultural Trust

*The royal drum (Bagyendanwa) being loaded on a lorry soon after the abolition of kingship (**Uganda Argus,** 28 September 1967)*

Mugaba palace at Kamukuzi, Mbarara, in ruins

John Barigye at his coronation in 1993, which was subsequently nullified by the NRM government

Kesi Nyakimwe, the chairman of Banyankore Cultural Foundation which is opposed to the restoration of Obugabe in Ankole

6
Institutionalisation and Institutional Relevance

We have seen that the Ankole kingship lost its distinctive functions and encountered formidable obstacles in developing new ones. There have appeared good grounds to argue that in the process the institution became redundant and in the end could be easily pushed aside. Let us now ask what lessons, if any, we might learn from this experience. Is such a process a retrogressive one, to be regarded with consternation and dismay; should it be viewed as modernisation and progress –or as what indeed?

Naturally, answers to many such questions tend to be inspired by taste or political preference. But in the last resort they also hinge – or better: should hinge – on the kind of criteria one chooses to employ in assessing the staying power, or the staying 'need', of institutions. In saying this, there is of course a good chance that one merely paraphrases the question, for consensus on yardsticks seems by no means assured. But even then–or especially then–the issue of criteria seems crucial.

In the voluminous but short-lived literature on political development, institutionalisation has frequently been put forward as a strategy, and as a yardstick for evaluation. 'Structures' must be seen to be transforming into 'institutions'; where such processes obtain 'political development' is said to be forthcoming. Again, as mentioned at the beginning of this book, often the same imperative is implied in certain themes of anthropology as well as of public administration and political sociology.[1] Perhaps most emphatic of all, practitioners of the sub-field labelled 'organisational development' would maintain that to institutionalise, i.e., to strengthen organisational structures against 'turbulent' environment, is a *sine qua non*.

Now, it goes without saying that institutionalisation is something different from institutional decline and redundancy. Quite clearly these two notions are diametrically opposed. But precisely because they are so, it should logically follow that if a positive value is attached to institutionalisation, then institutional decline should be negatively assessed. Again, therefore, in a case as that of Ankole's kingship, should that be our conclusion?

It is evident that normative generalisations about institutionalisation need indeed to be critically considered. Truly enough, in today's world there are numerous instances of institutional decline and rupture and quite likely very many of these are indices of 'something' problematic. It is plain that if all such discontinuities would need to be viewed with apprehension, the emergent picture would be rather bleak. Still, no matter how problematic some cases, there yet appears no convincing theoretical ground for any general view of institutional breakdowns as matters of regression, decay, or any other *a priori* negative assessments. Institutional patterns or developments, including breakdowns, are problematic given certain assumptions–such as that institutional strength in, by, or for itself is a desirable thing. But what may look ominous from one such perspective may hardly be problematic given other assumptions such as the premise that institutions are only worth maintaining if they can be expected to contribute to socially relevant goals.

Instead, it is not too difficult to see how a concept of institutionalisation *qua* concept may become overly prescriptive and can come to sustain, if not to contribute to, normative generalisations about the maintenance of institutions. For while on the one hand the concept connotes a process of reciprocal and progressive adjustment of politico-administrative practices and social norms – and thus 'change' of a sort – on the other hand it hardly addresses itself to broader societal changes, nor can it be easily related to the latter. It must be noted here that there is nothing in the concept which a *priori* excludes the possibility of institutionalisation keeping pace with, or even promoting, change within a broader context. But at the same time there is also nothing in the concept which draws primary attention to the ways in which institutions do or do not relate to societies in rapid or major social change.

A similar conceptual silence indeed obtains in regard to institutions of traditional authority, conceived as these have been as being embedded in cultural norms and values. Institutions of this kind are presupposed to command supportive social orientations but clearly this can only go as long as the 'norms and values' (whatever they are) are not themselves subject to change. Again, therefore, there is a similarly implicit assumption of 'social stability' to this notion of institutions, one which all too often seems unwarranted in the light of reality situations.

The issue thus partly boils down to a matter of perceptions. While stability may be, and indeed is, desirable from various points of view, existence of such preferences is immaterial to the cardinal fact that ongoing social change happens to be characteristic of most contemporary situations. Consequently, concepts concerned with entities that are placed in the midst of such change, but which as concepts would turn a deaf ear to precisely that dimension, inevitably tend to be hampered by a certain lack of fit in dealing with reality.

Ankole kingship in retrospect

In retrospect, we must now reconsider the decline and eclipse of Ankole kingship. Evidently, some of the general observations made in the previous chapter reach beyond the kind of problematics experienced by the Ankole monarchy as an institution in decline. Nonetheless, some lessons may well be drawn by relating their implications to this specific experience. Already, the case appears to underscore that what applies to concepts of institutions may hold for institutions themselves: not a few institutions have proven ill-adapted to transformations occurring around them, and consequently face either challenge or collapse. In several ways this indeed appears to have been true for Ankole kingship. In such an event, then, rather than lament 'it should not have happened', it suggests itself again that consideration of retention or discontinuation of an institution must primarily rest on its (present or potential) societal relevance which today more likely than not is to be tested in an environment that is subject to major change.

Is it in this vein, then, that we should judge the decline and eclipse of Ankole kingship? Much of the evidence goes to suggest so. We have seen the major colonial transformations to which the institution was subject and we have noted the unspectacular exit of the monarchy at the time of its abolition. Clearly, the transformations it was faced with were manifold, drastic, and largely concurrent, and it is indeed difficult to see how any institution whose role was so evidently rooted in a different historical context could have overcome them. Neither the expansion of scale of Ankole nor the kingdom's incorporation into Uganda were particularly conducive to a continued meaningful role of the kingship or to a successful search for new relevance. The same was true, as indeed we have seen, for the redefinition of the sociopolitical context of the Obugabe – the reduction of Bahinda influence and the increasingly tenuous Bairu-Bahima division. Perhaps most clearly of all, the organisational role (or lack of it) which the Omugabe was given to play in the colonial framework was ridden with ambiguities and manifestly failed to provide or allow for a meaningful involvement. Thus, the lack of reaction to the abolition of Ankole kingship did not seem very surprising; it rather tended to confirm and exemplify the extent of unrelatedness that had grown between the kingship and Ankole society.

A case might now well be made for the argument that the Ankole kingship had become a redundant institution, whose discontinuation made no particular difference to the sociopolitical framework and process of Ankole. If we do this it will be evident that the argument must hinge largely, though not exclusively, on the accuracy of the lukewarm reactions evidenced at the time of the monarchy's abolition. This must be so because in the case of institutions which are largely expected to command popular allegiances (such as religious institutions and other symbolic structures) a test of institutional redundancy should particularly lie in the nature of the orientations which their presumed 'clienteles' exhibit towards them. Lack of power *per se* is therefore not necessarily a criterion of such redundancy. Clearly, as long as an institution has an impact, no matter how one evaluates this impact, it cannot be described as 'redundant'. Power and influence may be viewed or experienced in either positive or negative terms, but to talk of institutional redundancy only makes sense if such influence is lacking in either way. It is suggested, therefore, that an institution is redundant if it no longer serves an essential purpose within its sociopolitical context –in other words, if its presence or absence makes no difference to the overall social and political process.[2]

In the case of symbolic institutions such as the Ankole monarchy–and it is hard to see that any other role could be claimed for the Obugabe in its terminal years–their relevance or redundancy would thus need to be an expression of the extent to which people are knowledgeable of, identifying with, or indifferent towards these institutions, or else would plainly reject their role or existence. In this sense, then, institutional redundancy comes in as a variant, and a measure of assessment, of institutional decline. It does not essentially matter in this respect that there are normally only few issues on which an entire society unequivocally shares the same views. Anything like 'complete' redundancy is indeed an abstraction which in reality will be found in exceptional cases only; institutional redundancy in terms of popular allegiances, in other words, means no more nor less than that in some predominant measure that quality seems applicable. Again, however, in 1967 there was nothing to indicate that this was not the case with regard to Ankole kingship.

On the above basis we would indeed come to qualify the Ankole kingship as a redundant institution. But is that all? Beyond or before making such a qualification, which as understood is particularly reflective of the 1967 situation, we will need to consider two further aspects of the matter. The first requires that we look at the institution's role during the transformation of Ankole's sociopolitical context, not so much for the way in which these transitions impinged upon its own performance, but rather to see what its presence did (or did not do) to facilitate or otherwise affect the processes of change to which the society was subject. The second point is closely related and asks whether or not institutional decline and redundancy in this particular case may have correlated with, or resulted from, processes of growth or development in other directions.

As regards the first of these queries, on the basis of notions of political development which rest on criteria of institutionalisation, it can be argued that Ankole kingship was an institution in decay. In the same vein, some would consider it an example of political regression, not development. Strictly speaking, if the interest is purely in the fortunes of a specific institution, such a view cannot be disputed. Obviously, Ankole kingship did not 'develop' in the present century. By some of the standards we have seen above, Ankole kingship definitely was not a case of political development; it lacked the conditions for an effective search of new goals, it did not exhibit an increase in functional complexity, and its longevity in the end was thwarted.

Again, however, the question remains how useful it is to employ such a yardstick. The functions of the Ankole monarchy were eroded when a new and more inclusive organisational framework was imposed upon the society. Basically, there was no compelling requirement for a role of kingship in that framework. But since there happened to be a monarchy in Ankole, its retention suggested itself at least on the ground that a premature decapitation might generate popular reactions which could hamper the development of an effective administration. In point of fact, while the monarchy was made to shed its functions one by one, its continuation during the establishment of new political and administrative structures probably helped obviate an abrupt legitimacy crisis. Its own problems and ambiguities were no less severe when serving that purpose, however; indeed these problems were rendered all the more acute by the process of self-liquidation to which the kingship found itself subjected. The main significance of the Ankole monarchy was that it acted as a thin shell for transformation. It helped to define the cognitive map of many members of Ankole society at a time when major transitions were under way. As these transformations were reaching completion, the shell could be finally thrown away.

Thus, it appears that the Ankole monarchy was useful while losing its functions, or in a sense relevant while growing redundant. Indeed the connection perhaps was even more immediate: its growing redundancy may well have been a 'relevant' factor in the light of the widening Bairu-Bahima division, preventing the occurrence of more direct political confrontation between the two groups. But did the kingship's decline also correlate with 'growth' or 'development' in any other ways? Again, this must be a matter of judgment and criteria, which in fact throws up one of two key caveats which seem to remain when reviewing the monarchy's fortunes over the present century. If we are merely to look for features of growth, such as the expansion, proliferation and increasing diversity of administrative and political structures, roles and regulations, then by all means the tendency in Ankole has been an 'upward' one over the years. Even if we were to employ some of the indices which have been frequently advanced for purposes of assessing 'political development', such as increasing specificity and differentiation of political and administrative roles and an expanding scope of tasks which a politico-administrative system is capable of undertaking, then again chances are we would conclude that the Ankole experience was meeting these yardsticks.

Thus, if we left it there, we might not just see a correlation of the phenomena of administrative growth and the eclipse of the Ankole kingship, but it could be argued that the monarchy's decline was a result and an accelerator of these institutional changes on a wider scale. In this sense, then, the role of the Ankole kingship, even as a declining institution, could conceivably be related to 'growth' and 'development'. The example would underscore that limited utility is to be gained by analysing institutions in isolation for assessing 'political development', and suggest that the elimination of a superfluous institution may itself be regarded as an instance of such development. In its broadest sense, the case would illustrate a universal phenomenon, namely, that growth processes throw up redundancy.

Still, two caveats remain when drawing these conclusions, and they are of no small importance. One was already alluded to and indeed was to be anticipated in the first place. The other as we will see evolved from a somewhat unexpected development and in fact was not without an element of surprise. Both raise open, though for that matter no less fundamental questions.

As regards the first of these issues, the point of this book essentially has been that the colonial framework imposed upon Ankole society pushed out the monarchy as a relevant institution. In the structures for colonial control and transformation which permeated the society little room was left for the kingship. Its social context, moreover, was drastically changed as political divisions tended to further reduce its role. Consequently, the institution became increasingly superfluous and irrelevant. After Uganda's independence these tendencies did not change but instead were drawn to their logical conclusion.

Now, without trying to belabour the obvious, it should be quite clear that the redundancy of Ankole's kingship was determined by the colonial framework and indeed came to constitute institutional irrelevance in terms of that framework. Quite specifically, therefore, the monarchy's decline was contextually determined. As noted also, the colonial framework embodied growth of some kind – the nature of which does not need to be detailed here. But few people now would consider such growth development in any stricter sense. Any colonial welfare and benefits to incorporated populations in most instances came as by-products of other objectives, political as well as economic ones. It was these which were paramount and followed from the dictates of metropolitan policies; colonial operations were simply not primarily motivated by concern with the interests of annexed societies.

While clearly this must be borne in mind when regarding the nature of the framework which eroded the Ankole monarchy, there is also another aspect to consider. Today, the legacy of institutional structures and bureaucratic attitudes in many ex-colonial countries is such that increasingly the arrangements of these structures themselves are being regarded as a major constraint on development efforts. Put starkly, many inherited organisational frameworks appear not so much irrelevant but dysfunctional instruments in terms of the declared purposes of development policies. Still, it was largely through the establishment and proliferation of such structures that an institution such as the Ankole monarchy came to lose its essential meaning and purpose. Though this does not alter the kingship's decline and increasing lack of relevance, it is nonetheless difficult to regard it as an example of obsolescence at the hands of patterns of 'progress'. Rather, a summing up might be that a once functional institution was eroded by dysfunctional arrangements – Gresham's law applied to politics.

Lastly, a rather unexpected development as mentioned threw up a second caveat, which from another angle again raised the question of institutional relevance. It will be recalled that in January 1971, a few years after the abolition of monarchical institutions in Uganda, an army coup overthrew the Obote government and put General Idi Amin in power. During the first few months of his presidency the general evidently faced a need to cultivate sources of support in addition to the backing of the soldiers who had helped put him in power. Spending little time in the office, for a considerably period he extensively toured the country, addressing public gatherings and engaging in discussions with 'Elders' (a newly coined category of hand-picked notables assumed to represent public opinion in each district) about the problems which concerned them. Many of the policy statements which thus emerged seemed to assume that Uganda's problems had been largely caused by the previous regime: on issue after issue where the Obote government had said 'yes', Amin's government would say 'no' (or vice versa) in an attempt to establish its credibility.

One step for which Obote's government was, of course, vividly remembered was its abolition of the monarchies. From the outset, however, this happened to be a matter for which the new regime did not want to change the beacons. One of the '18 points' the soldiers had submitted upon their January 1971 takeover was that Uganda was to remain a republic. Nonetheless, there continued to be strong feelings about the matter among the neo-traditional Baganda elite, a category which was of no small concern to Amin in his efforts to gain popularity and support. The Baganda elite had felt hurt through the loss of status and influence they had suffered during the Obote years, so much of which had seemed symbolised by the Kabaka's deposition. At the same time, to Amin they appeared as a powerful force to contend with.

Once installed, one of Amin's first moves did a great deal to get the Baganda on his side: he had the body of Sir Edward Mutesa, the late Kabaka deposed by the Obote government, flown over from London and given a state funeral in Uganda. Also, the Kabaka's relatives received various kinds of compensation and at not a few public occasions a deliberate limelight was put on them, particularly on Ronald Mutebi, the late Kabaka's son. Gestures of a somewhat similar conciliatory nature were also made towards the ex-rulers of the other abolished kingdoms of Uganda, whom Amin used to meet from time to time during the first half year or so of his government. The political climate seemed to be changing and to open up for a reconciliation with (neo-) traditional leadership.

Then, the inevitable question was raised. The Baganda 'elders', stimulated by Amin's policies of reversal, asked for the restoration of the Kabakaship. When first commenting on the request, the general did not flatly say 'no'. Possibly anticipating a promise of political goodwill, he instead congratulated the Baganda elders ontheir frankness and responded that the issue was a very important one which required careful study of all aspects, especially costs. Also, he added, opinions from all the districts of Uganda would have to be made clear on the matter before it could be further considered.[3]

With this, the Baganda began to see a possibility of their case being won. The new government appeared ready to reconsider the question of kingship. The main thing necessary seemed to be for the right kind of representations to be put forward. If all groups respectful of tradition could be mobilised, monarchies would be restored to their true standing.

Uganda for a short spell thereafter experienced one of its most lively and interesting recent discussions. The government had called for public debate on the question of restoration. In response, during August and September 1971, memorandum after memorandum was produced and submitted to the general by the elders of each district. Three of these, of the elders of Ankole, Buganda and Kigezi summarise a good deal of the flavour of the discussions and are reproduced herewith as Appendices I, II and III respectively. Virtually every conceivable argument pro or con was presented. As it happened, however, the pros emanated almost exclusively from the Baganda quarters. For lack of consensus or even a beginning of majority opinion, therefore, the issue soon dwindled as rapidly as it had arisen.

Part of this episode's interest for a retrospective look at Ankoie kingship lies nonetheless in the arguments which were advanced on the possible restoration of monarchical institutions. As can be seen from their memorandum, the Ankole representatives among other things stressed the need to curb factionalism, costs, unwanted exaltations, and divided loyalties in opposing such restoration. Significantly, some of these arguments had earlier been heard at the time of the abolition of the kingships. In contrast, the Buganda memorandum naturally offered a different kind of story, which is of interest precisely on that account. Due in part to their social and political affinities, the Kigezi arguments were again closely akin to those of Ankole, opposing restoration of the monarchies partly on the ground that they had lost their functions and relevance.

At the same time, the Ankole memorandum also derived a special significance from the cross-section of political leadership which endorsed it. In the light of the prolonged rivalry for influence which had been taking place in the district political arena, it was quite remarkable that leaders of Bahima and Bairu, of Protestants, Catholics and Muslims, and even of the factions which formerly were opposed within the Uganda People's Congress, for once appeared jointly as the signatories to a statement pleading against the restoration of kingship.

Still, the Ankole memorandum's greatest significance lay perhaps not in its argumentation or even its endorsement, but in the fact that the representatives who submitted it to General Amin included Ankole's ex-Omugabe, Gasyonga II. This rather unique fact – an ex-king requesting the non-restoration of kingship – appears important no matter which of two possible motivations might have been at play: whether it was Gasyonga's own will and initiative to be included among the party, or whether others had pressed him to lend his name to it. In either case, what mattered was the effort made to legitimise the continued abolition of Ankole kingship by enlisting the ex-monarch's support for it. That effort seemed to point to one last question: was the Ankole kingship yet not without relevance?

Notes

1   The institution-building school or movement is of particular interest in this regard. For a recent introduction, see Joseph W. Eaton (ed.), *Institution Building and Development, From Concept to Application*, Beverly Hills/London, 1972. The theoretical contributions of Esman should here be singled out for their recognition and stress of the need for societal relevance of institutions. See e.g. Milton I. Esman and Fred C. Bruhns, 'Institution Building in National Development: An Approach to Induced Social Change in Transitional Societies', in Hollis W. Peter (ed.), *Comparative Theories of Social Change,* Ann Arbor, 1966.

2   However different, this is not necessarily opposed to the notion of redundancy in Martin Landau, 'Linkage, Coding, and Intermediacy: A Strategy for Institution-building', *Journal of Comparative Administration,* Vol. 2, no. 4, 1971. Landau writes: 'A network of parallel linkages [can] provide a duplication of channels so that if transfer is not effected at one point, it can still be had at others. A redundancy of code and linkage is crucial to institutional development, and, when reinforced by duplicate or overlapping intermediate agencies, the possibilities of success are increased.' (424-425).

The difference here is one of terminology. If there is some utility to a structure, organisation or other element, then we would not call such an element 'redundant'. Rather, one might regard as 'redundant' such extra elements which happen to lack utility or function within their social environment. Institutional redundancy in this sense may be illustrated by the civil servant who, without anybody being aware of it, kept himself occupied year in year out putting certain stamps on certain forms. One day, as the story goes, a lion made his way into the office and ate the man, but the latter's disappearance was not noticed until several years later when he failed to respond to a pay-roll check.

3   *Uganda News,* no. 3569/71, 6 August 1971.

7
The New Politics of Kingmaking*

with Frederick Mwesigye

Uganda today offers a remarkable demonstration of the dynamics of cultural identity and political power. Following prolonged pressures from monarchist circles in Buganda, measures were initiated in 1993 to allow the restoration of ceremonial forms of kingship in three of the four former kingdom areas, namely Buganda, Bunyoro and Toro. These four ex-kingdoms, including Ankole, had been abolished in 1966-7 by President Obote, following a head-on collision with the central kingdom, Buganda, and its Kabaka (king). What was meant to be a purely cultural institution, however, soon began to acquire important political attributes. The Buganda *Lukiiko* (council), while accepting the position that the Kabaka should be a traditional ruler and should not be involved in politics, insists that the Kabaka should have, in addition to the *Lukiiko,* his own government with ministers appointed for specific assignments.[1] Similarly, the Omukama of Toro, Patrick Kaboyo, soon after his reinstallation took the initiative of designating 'ministers' for specific assignments.[2] A fair amount of complexity arose as the issue concerned not one but several kingdoms, with vastly different implications for each of them, while moreover there was no question of restoring any monarchical status *of* a state *within* the state of Uganda. Most important, however, is the vexed question as to what exactly was being proposed to begin with: restoration of a purely cultural, but strictly non-political role for traditional rulers, as the National Resistance Movement (NRM) would want to see it, or ultimately a fuller constitutional role with prerogatives that have yet to be sorted out.

The restoration issue acquired prominence in the course of 1993 when Uganda moved towards the finalisation of its constitution-making process and began preparing for the Constituent Assembly elections. The choice between a multi-party political system or a no-party system, in the latter case with an extension of NRM rule by another five years, had emerged as one of the key issues in that process. The prolongation of the NRM rule by electoral mandate could become a possibility if, in addition to its own popularity in the west of the country, it could also count on support from Buganda. Political negotiators

---

* This chapter is an updated version the one originally published as chapter 4 in Holger Bernt Hansen & Michael Twaddle (eds), 1995, *From Chaos to Order: The Politics of Constitution Making in Uganda*, Kampala: Fountain Publishers.

on behalf of Buganda appeared ready to provide this support, if in turn they could be assured that the restoration of the position of the Kabaka would be put on the agenda. *Ebyaffe* – 'our things' -– became the popular expression for what they wanted.

With this understanding, which lay at the basis of a constitutional amendment passed by the National Resistance Council (NRC) in July 1993 to allow the 'unbanning' of traditional rulers, the possibility for the return of kingship became a fact. The possible implications of this arrangement for the future state of (political) affairs in Uganda were many. In this chapter, we shall in particular try to explore the implications of Buganda's *Ebyaffe* for the rest of the country.

Background

To better appreciate these issues, it is important to bear in mind the historical background. One aspect of this is that at various points in the colonial and post-colonial periods, there have been confrontations between Buganda and the central government. Buganda, as the largest, richest and centrally located of the four kingdoms within Uganda, could and occasionally did present a direct challenge to the central government. At the core of these confrontations lay the question as to how much autonomy Buganda was to enjoy. In several of these confrontations, the Kabaka played a central role, supported largely by traditionalist elements based in land property and chiefly positions and drawn largely from Protestant circles. Parallel (but not unrelated) to this, there has often been a 'Buganda versus the rest' sentiment playing a role in Uganda politics.

Thus, when considering the pressures from monarchist Baganda circles to be allowed to revive their Kabakaship, it should be clear that the 'unbanning' in their case meant a good deal more than rehabilitation of hurt pride at the abrupt dismantlement of the kingdom of Buganda in 1966-7, although that, too, was a significant factor. Since that time, Baganda elites had been acutely aware that ultimate power in the country lay elsewhere: in the north under Obote, Amin and again Obote II, and then in the west with Museveni's National Resistance Army. Though not exactly a pursuit of national unity, therefore, the very presence and the symbolic institutional roles a Kabaka could play tended to be perceived by these strata in terms of strengthening Buganda's position and identity *vis*-à-*vis* the central government and the rest of Uganda.

Moreover, with the Kabaka reinstalled, it was hoped to reconstitute Buganda (subdivided into districts following the 1966 crisis) as a distinct entity around him, based on federalism. It was also hoped that these steps might add up to the restoration of the hegemony of a Protestant Baganda elite. However, there was a significant range of variation even among the Baganda. To liberal Baganda monarchists, Baganda could afford to lose part of its pre-1967 status while consolidating itself. Several groups in Buganda, including the historically annexed entities of Koki and Buruli as well as a critical NRM group, were actually opposed to the idea of restoration.[3] Radical Baganda monarchists – the *Bazzukulu ba Buganda* – however, wanted to settle for nothing less than restoration of Buganda's full status as per the 1900 Buganda Agreement, and for a Kabaka with actual constitutional powers.

While Buganda has to some extent recovered its pre-1967 status, it is quite clear that what has been revived is not so much the culture of Buganda but rather the potential power of culture in the political process. One key factor was the return to the Kabaka of the 350 square miles of land of which he was the titular owner and the obligatory rent and rates on this land from the tenants. The land connection is more of a political-economic nature than a cultural one, and is likely to strengthen and consolidate the position of the Kabaka, and the offices around him, within the wider politico-institutional setting.

The *Ebyaffe* that Buganda has persistently demanded from the central government were not clearly defined. In 1955, Buganda signed an agreement with the colonial authorities before Kabaka Mutesa II was released from exile. The agreement made the Kabaka constitutional head of Buganda and provided for election of the *Lukiiko* by universal suffrage. Buganda attached and still does attach great significance to this event. Buganda clashed with the central government over this issue in 1966. The restored monarchy in Buganda is supposedly a 'cultural' one. But the *Ebyaffe* the Buganda monarchists have always been fighting for are in no way cultural only. For this reason, the Baganda became increasingly opposed to the draft constitutional proposals for a unitary republican government.

The western kingdoms

Compared to Buganda, the other three former kingdoms, Ankole, Bunyoro and Toro, had never posed a challenge to the centre. Without denying their historical roots (but neither ignoring how drastically they were transformed and reshaped during colonial rule), their roles and positions were very much derived from what happened to Buganda. In a sense, if there had been no Buganda, there probably would not have been much reason for the colonial strategists or their successors to bother much about the exact status of Ankole, Toro or Bunyoro. If there had been no revival of the monarchy in Buganda, there probably would have been no one particularly concerned with Ankole, Toro or Bunyoro. But during the colonial period, as Buganda somehow had to be accommodated within the larger framework, some similar form of accommodation was designed for the other three as well. As already mentioned in this book, at the time of Ankole's incorporation into colonial Uganda, for example, the kingdom was expanded to several times its original size, presumably to help offset the territorial preponderance Buganda had gained. Similarly, Toro's expansion and incorporation of the Rwenzori areas was promoted. Bunyoro, on the other hand, was cut short as a penalty for its opposition to British Imperialism, and to the benefit of Buganda.

Again, in preparation of a constitutional framework for independence, the recognition and inclusion of four traditional kingdoms within the framework of Uganda could seemingly reduce Buganda to a position of just one out of four. But when Buganda conflicted with the central government in 1966 and was dismantled as a kingdom, the other three had to go as well. The reaction at the time, it would be well to remember, was hardly one of shock: there was pervasive indifference, and occasionally joy at the abolition of the traditional rulers. Nonetheless, in 1993 it appeared opportune to the NRM government to accommodate the wishes of Baganda royalist circles to have their Kabaka reinstated; it seems to have been taken for granted that the same should happen in the other three cases, or even in other places 'if', as the NRM put it, 'the people so wish'.

The 'if the people so wish' clause in the monarchical restoration bill and in the 1995 constitution was not without consequence. First, it sparked off an interest in reinstatement of traditional rulers in some other parts of Uganda like Busoga, Acholi and Nebbi, while in other cases it prompted a new wave of 'wanting to be on a par' with Buganda. Thus, for some areas of northern Uganda, the formation of a state within the state of Uganda was proposed[4] in order to acquire a status comparable to that of Buganda when negotiating with the central government, while there was also a call for the recognition of Lango as a state within the future framework of Uganda. The Buganda Lukiiko made a further appeal to this logic with its proposal to the Constituent Assembly to constitute Uganda into a fourteen-state federal state, sparking off a new debate between supporters of 'federalism' and of 'decentralisation'.[5]

Significantly, amidst all the attention Uganda devoted to the coronation of Buganda's new Kabaka in 1993, representatives from the other three ex-kingdoms in the NRC discovered that the bill drafted for the 'unbanning' of traditional rulers referred to all the kingdoms, not just to Buganda which had been negotiating for it.[6] There had been no demand for it from the districts concerned and as far as the Ankole case was concerned, the district resistance committees of Mbarara and Bushenyi had actually opposed the idea of reinstatement. Critical opponents from these and other areas in the NRC put up fierce opposition but failed to get the applicability for the bill limited to Buganda, nor did they succeed in getting an amendment accepted that would make the restoration of kingship subject to popular referendum.

But the role and significance of kingship especially in Ankole and Toro had been historically vastly different from that in Buganda and several quite problematic issues were likely to arise here. The reinstatement of Toro kingship was a rather ambiguous proposition as the monarchy had been very controversial within the former kingdom of Toro. Among the Batoro proper, the royal entourage drew and still presumably draws its main support from more narrowly circumscribed circles and areas, such as Mwenge. Nearly half the population incorporated into the Toro kingdom, however, consisted of Bakonzo and Baamba, on the border of the Democratic Republic of Congo, who felt they had been unjustly included in Toro and had been treated as second-class citizens by its government. From 1961 onwards the Bakonzo and Baamba staged a prolonged and bitter struggle (the Rwenzururu rebellion) to get separated from Toro.[7] One section of the Bakonzo at one point even established their own 'independent' Rwenzururu kingdom, which lasted for several years. During Amin's time, two separate districts were created for the Bakonzo and Baamba to help cool down their main grievances. Therefore, they are now only prepared to consider the reinstated Omukama as ruler over the Batoro, the core population group of the former kingdom, but they are wary about any possible claims of authority over the other former sections of the population. In the wake of the present revival of kingship in Uganda, the Rwenzururians have declared that they would also revive their own kingship and duly warned the Omukama of Toro to keep off their declared 'kingdom'.[8]

Theoretically, the restoration of Toro kingship could indeed have referred to the boundaries of the former Toro kingdom thus again comprising Bakonzo, Baamba and other non-Batoro. A hint of such a claim was evident in the Omukama's reported intention to appoint some selected Bakonzo among his new ministers.[9] Any attempt at territorial restoration, however, was bound to provoke serious trouble in Kasese and Bundibugyo districts. During the 14 July 1993 NRC meeting, the government was warned that it should not become responsible for 'another Rwenzururu rebellion'.[10] This was followed by serious agitation in the Kasese area against tentative claims over the salt-rich Lake Katwe by the reinstalled Omukama of Toro, which traditionally had constituted a source of revenue for his government. This agitation, which was echoed in the NRC sessions by the Kasese representatives, vehemently opposed the provisions of the *Ebyaffe* bill returning all the cultural sites and other assets belonging to traditional rulers. Since then the salt lake area has been under the authority of the Kasese administration. Although the Toro kingship has been reinstated, it has lost much of its former significance and appeal as a result of the 'secession' of Bundibugyo and Kasese districts.

Finally, in the Bunyoro case there did not seem to be an overwhelming enthusiasm for the revival of monarchism in the first place. Instead, what followed the 'unbanning' act were prolonged succession disputes, which became partly associated with political party rivalries[11] and, among other things, meant that the Banyoro monarchists were not able to lobby the electorate in favour of pro-monarchy delegates to the Constituent Assembly. The dispute was centred upon the will of the late Omukama, Sir Tito Winyi, and involved two contenders, both from the royal Babiito clan, Prince John Mpuuga Rukidi and Prince Solomon Iguru. The matter was settled in a High Court ruling in favour of Prince Iguru, who thus became Bunyoro's 27th Omukama.

The Ankole case

Of the various monarchical restoration questions in Uganda, the Ankole case clearly has become the most controversial one. In fact, in view of very strong opposition to the revival of kingship in the former Ankole kingdom area, its restoration has so far not materialised, although a coronation of the prince-heir, John Barigye, secretly took place in November 1993 but was subsequently declared invalid by the NRM government.

Among several contentious issues surrounding the restoration question in Ankole, the most important one is that in the past, specifically during the colonial period, Ankole kingship had been associated with a pattern of ethnic inequality (in terms of political power, chiefly positions, initial educational advantages) between an elite stratum of Bahima and the large majority of Bairu peasants.[12] Though Ankole kings were drawn from the Bahinda clan which theoretically was distinct from both Bahima and Bairu, in reality kingship for all intents and purposes was identified with the Bahima. As Dr Barya put it while addressing the question why the Banyankore reject the return of the Omugabe, 'Monarchism in Ankole evokes centuries of oppression and domination by the Bahima in general but the Bahinda in particular over the Bairu majority in Ankole.'[13] Since many Banyankore would thus see the kingship as a symbol of past ethnic subordination, resistance against its reintroduction became very fierce indeed.

As already mentioned, Ankole was a colonial creation from the former Nkore kingdom which was expanded to over twice its size by the inclusion of Buzimba, Buhweju, Bunyaruguru, Igara, parts of the former kingdom of Mproro and most of Sheema as a result of British rule. This expansion has been looked at by several Banyankore scholars as an extension of domination by Nkore, and one opinion has strongly argued that if kingship is to be revived in Ankole at all, it should not include those areas that were unwillingly incorporated.

Another controversy revolves around whether Prince Barigye is the rightful heir to the throne. Although there have not been any succession disputes among the royal house of Ankole, some scholars from Ankole have challenged his claim to the throne. Since there is no immediate dispute among the royal clan, however, it is probably fair to say that the legitimacy argument is mainly used to strengthen the opposition to restoration.

The ambiguities surrounding the restoration of kingship in Uganda have caused heated debate in Ankole on the question as to whether culture and kingship can be considered synonymous. Pro-restoration advocates argue that kingship was and is of the essence of Nkore culture, and that its restoration therefore is a *sine qua non*, culturally speaking. Opponents of restoration, on the other hand, say that there is no one-to-one relation between kingship and culture, citing the example of French culture that kept thriving even after the monarchy was terminated.[14]

In connection with the restoration question, there has been the birth of two bodies in Ankole, both purportedly working for the revival of Ankole culture. The first of these, the Nkore Cultural Trust, was founded mainly by Banyankore monarchists. For the Trust, although it sought to revive the culture of the Banyankore, culture was only to be the launching pad for the restoration of kingship in Ankole, just as it had been the case in Buganda. Significantly, the crown prince, John Barigye, became and still is the patron of the Trust. Whereas other members of the executive body of the Trust are elected, its patron is not. The Trust soon became solely preoccupied with the question of restoring the Ankole monarchy, with its patron leading a personal campaign towards this end. Drawing its membership from amongst the supporters of monarchism, the Trust has opened up branches in several counties of the former Ankole, especially in Mbarara district, and has elected representatives from each sub-county.

The second organisation is the Banyankore Cultural Foundation, which similarly has the promotion of Ankole culture as its rallying point. The Foundation, however, stringently separates the question of culture and kingship and would maintain that large (annexed) areas of Ankole did not have a monarchical culture to begin with. The Foundation was set up in a counter move, which is not uncommon in Ankole politics and, similar to the Trust, draws its active support largely from the educated urban elite.

Both the Foundation and the Trust claim to have a majority of support in Kampala and other towns of Uganda, in which they organise meetings and seek to strengthen their position. But whereas the Trust and the Foundation both draw much of their direct support from urban-based cadres, the Foundation relies heavily on Bairu membership (though Bahima are welcome) and almost certainly can count on substantial popular support in the densely populated areas of Sheema and Igara, while the Trust to a certain extent has cut across the ethnic Bahima/Bairu division, but may not be able to mobilise as large a popular following as the Foundation.

The disagreement that put the monarchists and the government into a deadlock came to a head with the clandestine coronation of Prince John Barigye as the Omugabe of Ankole. It is worth noting in this connection that Ankole is the home of many NRM leaders, including President Yoweri Museveni himself. Indeed, the core of NRM cadres in Ankole comprises leading figures from Bairu as well as Bahima backgrounds, and it was in fact their common involvement in the NRM which had given them the conviction that the ethnic distinctions of the past had been overcome. Ankole's kingship, however, used to be ethnically ascribed and could easily become a source of conflict. Knowing quite well the complexities that kingship would provoke in Ankole, the NRM government therefore wisely put the jig-saw puzzle before the Ankole monarchists by asking them to make consultations about its restoration with the would-be subjects of King Barigye. Earlier, however, the RC V representatives of Mbarara and Bushenyi districts had already presented two separate memoranda to the Constitutional Commission rejecting the restoration of the institution of kingship in Ankole. It therefore would be quite an uphill task to consult the people through the RC structure. In the minds of the monarchists this demand was uncalled for. Matters of people's culture, the monarchists argued, do not call for government permission allowing them to accept or practise it.

Thus, seemingly indifferent to the NRM politics, the Ankole monarchists on 20 November 1993 crowned Prince Barigye as the 22nd Omugabe of Ankole, some four months after the high profile coronation of Prince Ronald Mutebi as the 36th Kabaka of Buganda. The coronation ceremony had been publicised as the last funeral rites of the late Omugabe of Ankole, Charles Gasyonga II, so as to keep the initiative a secret until it would be a *fait accompli*.

The Ankole restoration issue placed the NRM government in an awkward dilemma. For the NRM, the restoration of kingship in Buganda was a purely non-political, cultural matter, or at least that was what the outside world was made to believe. (In other respects, of course, the arrangement was of the utmost political significance.) If Baganda monarchists wanted to see the institution instead as a political one, they would be made to respect the limits laid down by NRM. When the case of Ankole cropped up, the NRM discovered something was going wrong. The Ankole monarchist lobby ostensibly asked for nothing but a cultural institution and in view of the Buganda precedent they did not see this as a matter requiring a popular vote. Prince Barigye in fact had been making a point of saying that he would refuse to have his candidature subjected to a referendum.[15] Nonetheless, the NRC's 'unbanning' order had specified 'if people so wish' and the local dissent and conflict to be expected was grave and would affect NRM's home support itself. Here therefore the matter became highly political and had to be handled as a sensitive issue.

Hence, immediately after the coronation of Prince John Barigye as Omugabe, the government declared it null and void. Subsequently, a meeting of the RCIII, IV and V representatives in Mbarara, Bushenyi and Ntungamo districts (which together constitute the former Ankole kingdom) was called by President Museveni, which was also attended by the parliamentary representatives of the area, government officials and the army generals who had attended the coronation ceremony of Prince Barigye. The meeting condemned the unauthorised coronation and probably averted very serious conflicts from erupting, though perhaps it did not finally resolve the kingship issue in Ankole.

Wider implications

When drawing up a provisional balance sheet of the new politics of kingmaking in Uganda, probably the first thing to note should be that a similar move would have been inconceivable ten or twenty years ago. During the 1960s and 1970s, in particular, the climate of the time was strongly nationalistic, and kingdoms within a state such as the four in Uganda tended to be perceived as divisive and anachronistic in an era committed to promoting national unity and development. In 1987 the political weather still seemed no different. The NRM then passed an anti-sectarian bill prohibiting reference to one's culture or one's 'tribe'.

Today the picture has changed. While the Movement government is obviously interested in maintaining political order and stability, Uganda's development strategies are not especially noted for stressing income redistribution among regions, the promotion of national standards and uniformities, or the integration of different regional economic activities into a broader framework. Uganda, like many African countries, has embraced decentralisation as one of the key parameters for its development policies. Districts are encouraged to make their own development plans and find their own resources, while foreign donors and investors are given a great deal of scope in developing locally specific programmes and modes of collaboration.

Giving room to opt for the reinstallation of traditional rulers somehow seems consistent with this climate and emphasis on decentralisation. Theoretically, this option might enhance a cultural dimension and local pride in the pursuit of decentralised development activities. However, emphasis on cultural specificities and traditional institutions also runs a danger of promoting chauvinistic sentiments and ethnically parochial, potentially intolerant outlooks. The dividing line between these two tendencies is often only a thin and fluid one. If culture becomes synonymous with having kings, for example, then there is every chance of a revival of pre-abolition stereotypes and feelings of superiority *vis-à-vis* groups without a royal tradition.

One question which appears to have received only limited attention in the discussions around the restoration of kingship is a simple but possibly far-reaching one, namely what territorial units do the respective kingships actually refer to? One answer to this might be that the restoration and the 1995 constitution do not provide a legal framework for territorial boundaries since they leave it open to people concerned to 'practise' their culture and pay homage to their particular traditional ruler, wherever or whoever they might be. However, this interpretation does not quite match the emerging practice, in which there are certainly references back to the original reach of the respective (ex) kingdoms, presumably with an intent of restoration in a territorial sense as well.

Before 1966 the picture was fairly straightforward: Buganda, Bunyoro, Toro and Ankole were all distinct units of government, each symbolically headed by monarchical institutions. Since then, Buganda has been split into thirteen districts, Toro into five and Ankole into three. In the Buganda case, restoration of the Kabakaship implied and facilitated devising ways of restoring the unity of its thirteen districts, the 'federalist' option. By implication this was likely to revive manifestations of a 'Buganda versus the rest' complex within Uganda. The decision by the Buganda *Lukiiko* to reinstate a whole range of self-governing functions for a Buganda government, under its titular head, the Kabaka, was expected to reinforce such trends.

In the Toro case, there is no conceivable way in which the reinstated kingship can actually reclaim a relation to two (Kasese and Bundibugyo) of the five districts into which the former kingdom of Toro has been subdivided. As noted above, there are attempts to foster alliances with groups and individuals within the lost districts, but these are unlikely to produce any widened basis of popular support. Practically, therefore, Toro jurisdiction is confined to Kabarole, Kamwenge and Kyenjojo districts.

In the Ankole case, again, the kingdom and later district by that name no longer exists. But theoretically the claims for restoration by the monarchist lobby – and similarly their refutation by its opponents – do refer to the whole of the former, undivided kingdom. The position of the Ankole monarchists thus is analogous to that of Buganda but rather different from that in Toro in the sense that they cannot settle for only a portion of the former kingdom area.

The Ankole dispute thus is remarkable in more than one sense. In the first place, it is not worthy that a place for kingship – whether cultural or political – is claimed (and, in turn disputed) with reference to an entity which has no contemporary institutional basis – and which, one might add, was pretty much a colonial fabrication to begin with. In this respect, the analogy to Buganda also hides an important difference: generally speaking the Buganda case has been much more homogeneous throughout, in terms of historical reference as well as degrees of popular support.

In the second place, the Ankole case is remarkable because, if it had been followed through, it would have entailed the reinstatement of a monarchical institution derived from a historical premise of ethnically determined hierarchical status. Thus, recognising the kingship would somehow have implied recognising an idea of ethnic inequality, with all the profound social and institutional consequences this might imply. It is not surprising therefore that representatives for the vast 'non-aristocratic' majority of the former kingdom should have put forward the argument that Kinyankore culture is not by definition a monarchically oriented culture, and that the equation of monarchy and culture is a far too narrowly conceived construct.

Conclusion

In conclusion one other point might be noted. The NRM government's decision to restore traditional rulers came at a time when there were repeated demands for lifting the 'ban' on political parties. Since 1986, when the NRM restored basic law and order in the south and west of the country and continued to fight and gradually win a civil war in the north and east, it has resisted the return of political parties on the grounds that they are divisive and potentially sectarian. The NRM's firmness on this point coincided with, and was partially an answer to, increasing calls for multi-party democratisation in Africa. Instead, the NRM introduced an alternative, 'non-party' way of electing representatives through the RC system, in which different echelons vote for representatives at the next higher level on an individual, non-party basis. In principle the Constituent Assembly elections opened the way for a discussion of, and choice between, adopting a multi-party system or continuing the present 'movement' system, but the comfortable majority returned from the west and south in favour of NRM's preferences on this score guaranteed that political parties would remain frozen. The 2000 referendum also reaffirmed the continuation of the 'movement system' at least for another five years. Instead of 'unbanning' political parties, the NRM allowed the 'unbanning' of traditional rulers, or at least of some of them. In the short run, this kept people's minds engaged on the pros and cons of reinstating kingship rather than on the merits and demerits of political parties. In the longer run, other possible – and possibly graver – divisions are at stake.

Uganda's complex and turbulent history is reflected in its record of constitution-making. The carefully worked out 1962 constitution and the abruptly tabled 1967 constitution represented two different responses, one federal, one unitary, to two central questions: the institution of kingship and the position of Buganda. Although the methods that led to the 1995 constitution were different from those of 1962 and 1967, the fundamental questions remained the same – kingship and Buganda. The consequence of this was that other basic issues, like the powers of the executives, the army, the police, the judiciary, and the organs for democratic representation, were left at the mercy of the tired minds of everybody after hustling with what was taken to be fundamental.

When trying to anticipate the longer-term implications of Uganda's restoration of monarchs, in the first place it seems this has been a crucial step in allowing the tabling of increasingly far-reaching claims for a distinct status and autonomy of Buganda, with the possibility of a corresponding gradual peripheralisation of the rest of the country. Within Buganda, the move seems to have been equally crucial in underpinning the claims for political hegemony of the Protestant Baganda elite, or conversely, the relegation of the Roman Catholic (DP) segment to a secondary position.

Outside Buganda, as noted, 'unbanning' created serious liabilities in terms of a good deal of ongoing controversy of different kinds in each of the other former kingdoms: succession disputes in Bunyoro; frustrated territorial restoration in Toro; and especially the problem of ethnic relations in Ankole. With respect to the non-kingdom areas, finally, the restoration of kingship may eventually entail the reassertion of stereo-typed images – about peoples with and without kings – in addition to their potential social and political marginalisation. Beyond this, larger questions about the country's longer-term cohesiveness and about different understandings of the added value of 'Uganda' are looming up. It is doubtful whether all the benevolent and traditional leadership roles expected of the reinstated monarchs will outweigh these various implications of *Ebyaffe*.

Notes

1 P. Mutibwa, 'Constitution-Making Process in Uganda: Ebyaffe-Necessary options for Peace and Freedom in Uganda. A paper presented at the conference on 'Combining Civic Peace with Civic Freedom: constitutional options of a New Uganda', Kampala, 1994.
2 *New Vision* 18 August 1993
3 *Ibid.*, 2 August 1993
4 *Ibid.*, 14 January 1994
5 *Daily Topic,* 4 May 1994
6 *The Monitor,* 23 July 1993
7 M. Doornbos, 'Kumanyana and Rwenzururu: Two Responses to Ethnic Inqeuality', in R.I, Rotberg and A.A. Mazrui (eds) *Protest and Power in Black Africa,* New York: Oxford University Press, 1970
8 *The Monitor,* 7 September 1993
9 *New Vision,* 7 September 19910.

10 *The Monitor,* 23 July 1993
11 *Weekly Topic I,* 5 November 1993
12 M. Doornbos. *Regalia Galore: The Decline and Eclipse of Ankole Kingship,* Nairobi: East African Literature Bureau, *1975*
13 *The Monitor,* 3 September 1993
14 E.g., the First Deputy Prime Minister E. Kategaya at the Karugire Memorial Debate, Makerere University, 14 October 1993
15 *New Vision,* 13 August 1993

8
Epilogue: Regalia Galore Revisited

The twentieth century ended on at least one unexpected note: in various parts of the world the possible re-entry of traditional rulers, or monarchy as an 'alternative' form of government, had come back on the agenda. How exactly this was to be explained was not entirely clear, and in due course this may well become one of those numerous topics left for debate among future historians. But if the apparent revival of interest in monarchism rested upon accurate observation, the evident question is why this was the case: was it to be explained as a reaction against 'globalisation', or disenchantment with the forms and performance of 'modern', 'secular', 'alienating' government? Was it a reflection of the end of the Cold War, or, generally, the 'post-modern condition'? Or did it constitute a search for and re-assertion of identity, in culturally specific terms, or some sub-conscious popular longing for imaginative roles and relationships, such as that between a prince and his people? Or else, perhaps, was it just plainly a reflection of media interests in having colourful parades and pageants (which are never the same with presidents or central committee chairmen not well groomed for such ceremonial events)?

Whatever the merits and demerits of these currents of thought and sentiment, the fact is that in a variety of contexts deposed monarchs or their descendants re-entered the limelight, revisited 'their' countries (often for the first time, though), and discreetly reminded governments and people alike that they were 'available'. This happened especially in the Balkans, though at one point the idea was floated even in a context as distant and unlikely as Brazil. Only in very few cases where heir pretenders thus re-appeared, however, did this lead to actual restoration so far. The Ugandan cases probably constituted the prime example of this happening. Close to the Ankole context, the new Tutsi-led regime in Rwanda has also been playing with the option of reinstating the Mwami, the Tutsi king. Still, irrespective of whether in the end these trends would materialise or not, the fact remains that monarchism once again was capturing imaginations – of all the people, or only of some. Moreover, the increasingly serious questioning of the future of monarchies in countries like Britain or the Netherlands tends to underscore the curiosity evoked by this trend outside the West.

Ankole constituted one of these sites where renewed attention was being given to the institution of kingship. Following the post-1986 sequence of events pertaining to the Ugandan kingships in general which has been described in

Chapter 7 of this book, the question of the return of Ankole kingship has been on the agenda as of the moment that restoration had appeared an option. The question had first been looked into by the Constitutional Commission which had been appointed by the National Resistance Movement government that had taken office in 1986. Based on extensive interviews with people from all walks of life and in all regions of Uganda, the commission had advised against re-opening the question of restoration of the Ankole monarchy as well as those of Bunyoro and Toro. In the light of its recommendations, a phrase was adopted in the draft constitution to the effect that monarchical restoration would be possible only 'if the people so wish'. With respect to the Ankole case, it appeared as if in taking this position, the commission was echoing the advice of the representation of Ankole elders, including the ex-Omugabe Gasyonga II, to President Idi Amin in 1971, which had warned that restoration of the kingship could become a seriously divisive issue (Cf. Appendix I, *Memorandum by the Elders of Ankole to the President, General Idi Amin Dada, on the Restoration of Kingdoms, August 1971*).

The 1995 constitution still makes reference to the 'wishes and aspirations of the people', but since the Kabaka of Buganda as well as the Abakama of Bunyoro and Toro were reinstated without a prior consultation procedure having been put constitutionally in place, the relevant clause now states different routes to restoration, i.e. 'the institution of traditional leader or cultural leader may exist in any area of Uganda in accordance with the culture, customs and traditions or wishes and aspirations of the people to whom it applies' (Uganda's Constitution, Ch. 16, Art. 246(2)[1]. It also stipulates, with an apparent reference to the Ankole stalemate, that 'in any community where the issue of traditional or cultural leader has not been resolved, the issue shall be resolved by the community concerned using a method prescribed by Parliament' (Ch. 16, Art. 246(2)). So far, however, the Uganda parliament has not yet laid down this procedure, which possibly reflects a lack of consensus on the matter even among the national legislators concerned.

Thus, the issue of the restoration of Ankole kingship was first tabled in 1993, but it has remained unresolved since then while continuing to engage proponents and opponents in numerous verbal battles, in the press as well as in the local and national arenas. Evidently, the question has been arousing deeply felt sentiments pro and against in Ankole, and in the process began to recreate rifts and antagonisms that one had previously assumed had been overcome. Kingship, which in essence one would expect to constitute a symbol of integration and unity, in Ankole was turning out to be an instrument of division and conflict.

It is rare to see a dispute of this kind emerge at the present time. Inevitably, it throws up a range of questions all at once: what triggered all this? why did supporters of the idea of restoration keep pressing their case as they saw it?

why did it engender such fierce resistance as it did? and how could this controversy have been avoided, if at all? To many onlookers within Uganda and outside, these appeared some of the initial puzzles and questions provoked by the dispute. Some stocktaking, partly in the light of the earlier analysis in *Regalia Galore* may, therefore, be pertinent in the search for answers. At the same time, a revisit to the original text should illuminate the extent to which orientations to the kingship and the climate of debate around the issue have changed.

Prima facie the proponents of restoration appeared to have quite a plausible case and argument. Ankole kingship had been abrogated in 1967 along with the three other monarchies that had been co-existing until then within independent Uganda, namely Buganda, Toro and Bunyoro. But whereas legitimacy had since been re-accorded, as of 1993, to the other three – mainly due to a powerful lobby that had been actively seeking the reinstatement of Buganda's monarchy – Ankole was still being kept waiting for it.

Restoration proponents submitted that the Ankole monarchy represented a precious historical institution of 600 years old, which therefore is well worth preserving as a crucial part of Ankole's cultural heritage.[3] Also, they saw re-institution of the monarchy as a way of re-creating a sense of corporate identity that might facilitate organisation for development projects of various kinds. Proponents could argue, as indeed they did, that the re-recognition of the legitimacy of Ankole kingship was implied in the very act which had re-established the other kingdoms within the country. Restoration having been accepted in principle by the government and ruling political circles, this would seem to suggest that having kings in these parts of Uganda had once again become the established norm. Not having a particular king back thus went against the norm, by that same logic.

Looked at from another angle, moreover, re-instituting only three of the four monarchies, but not the fourth, would seem to leave a conspicuous but uncomfortable-looking 'empty place', which would continue to raise questions, from outsiders if not from insiders. Also, the other (restored) rulers in Uganda might be found wondering why their fellow-monarch from Ankole was not being allowed to join in, and perhaps would feel his absence tended to qualify the irreversibility of their own restoration. Finally, behind these various sentiments and arguments there was no doubt also an expectation that ministerial and other roles, and indeed a whole complex of patronage relationships focused on the monarchy, could be created and recreated for the benefit of royalist supporters, as had meanwhile been happening elsewhere.

Yet, as will have become apparent from the preceding text, the Ankole case constitutes quite a special and complex one, defying easy categorisation and resolution. It derives its complexity less from the kingship question per se than from the historic social divisions between Bahima and Bairu within which it has been embedded as well as from the particular ways in which the institution has been reconstructed over time, notably during the colonial period. Unsurprisingly, several of these problematic aspects did get fiercely articulated in the opposition which the prospect of the monarchy's restoration has been engendering. In a sense, while there had been widespread indifference and some celebration in a few circles in response to the monarchy's abolition in 1967, by the year 2000 this indifference seemed to have been transformed into growing resistance to the idea of restoration, especially but not exclusively among Bairu. At the same time, it was also evident that groups favouring restoration felt no more restraints in the new political situation to expressing their demands and interests, and in effect turned out to have a remarkably vocal presence.

Thus, opponents of restoration could and did argue that Ankole's kingship largely represented a colonial creation, since more than half of the Ankole district as it had been (re-)constituted at the beginning of colonial rule consisted of (densely populated) areas which had never formed part of Nkore kingdom, Ankole's precursor entity. In fact, around 1900 Buhweju, Igara and Bunyaruguru were subdued and added to the new district of Ankole by force of arms[4]. Significantly, the 'colonial creation' argument was used to voice feelings of injustice done: other districts like Busoga had similarly been colonial creations with an amalgam of different elements thrown together, but as this did not engender perceived inequalities and resentment it did not prompt the same reservation and argument. In the case of Ankole, however, this historical reservation also led to one other counter-proposition: if restoration was to be contemplated at all, the question this raised was whether it should refer to the colonial institution or to the pre-colonial, historical, kingdom of Nkore. In the latter case, there would also be several other theoretical candidates for restoration, notably some of the smaller kingdoms that had been included into Ankole district at the beginning of colonial rule, like those of Buhweju, Igara and Kajara.

Restoration proponents took it for granted that reinstatement would concern the institution as it had been inherited from colonial times, not the pre-colonial Nkore kingdom and possible other candidates. Opponents of restoration argued that that would mean symbolically reinstating the extension of ethnically ascribed kingship, which had been experienced as discriminatory, over regions which historically had not formed part of its domain. They would also argue that in that case it would be difficult to maintain that the institution is 600 years old, as the Nkore Cultural Trust had claimed it to be. The colonially restructured institution had lasted only a little longer than 60 years, that is, from the time of the Ankole Agreement (1901) till its abolition in 1967. And, last but not least, they voiced their objection to the equation of Ankole culture with kingship, pointing to France and other examples as countries where culture was thriving after the termination of monarchism.

In this connection it is significant to note the historical differences regarding the position of kingship in Ankole society as contrasted to that of the other Ugandan monarchies. Specifically in terms of their embeddedness in the respective clan systems, there were notable differences between the position the Kabaka held within Buganda society as compared to that of the Omugabe within Nkore or Ankole. In Buganda, all Baganda in a way could consider the Kabakaship 'theirs', as the Kabaka in principle could marry from all 52 Buganda clans and thus derive an heir from any of them. In contrast, Ankole's kings (and historically Nkore's) were recruited exclusively from a single clan, that of the Bahinda. In terms of Ankole's ethno-social structure, the Bahinda as noted formed a minority among a minority, the Bahima, who in a number of ways were quite distinct from the majority of Banyankore. In the light of the historic relations of social distance and inequality that had existed between the Bahima elite and the Bairu, and strictly speaking also between Bahinda and Banyankore, opponents therefore argued that re-installing Ankole's kingship in effect would mean reinstating the symbolic pinnacle of Ankole's past ethnic inequality. It is this particular aspect which evidently represents the most profound strand of misgivings among many Banyankore with the idea of reviving the Ankole monarchy.

Against the background of these sensitivities, both the privately arranged coronation of Prince John Barigye as Omugabe of Ankole and its instant annulment by President Museveni in November 1993 produced immediate shock-effects within Ankole society. As to the coronation itself, it seemed telling that for the possible restoration of an institution that supposedly is a symbolic one, hence in principle belonging to the public domain and the public eye, one had sought recourse to a secretive if not clandestine coronation ceremony, away from popular scrutiny. The contradiction this implied in terms of what role the institution was to play, and how it was being perceived by those intimately connected with it, was quite astounding, and in final analysis appears tragically self-defeating.

The president's annulment of the coronation was instigated both by his role as guardian of the constitutional process, especially with the Constituent Assembly elections around the corner, and by his fear that the restoration would lead to the resurgence of ethnic animosity in his home region (which could seriously affect his own and the NRM's home support). Initially, his intervention appeared to have cooled down both the unease as well as expectations that had been aroused by the event. After the initial wave of consternation and relief had subsided, it seemed for a while as if the matter had been laid to rest in the face of the government's reiteration of its (constitutionally derived) position that the restoration of the monarchy was acceptable only 'if the people so wish'.

This lasted only for about a year, however. Thereafter, pressure and lobbying to try and make the government change its mind was resumed by the Nkore Cultural Trust (NCT), by Barigye himself, and by several high-ranking Uganda army officers from the region, and became ever more intense as time went by. Proponents of restoration protested that the 'if the people so wish' phrase was selectively applied to Ankole only, as the Constitutional Commission had not found majority support for restoration in the other ex-kingdoms outside Buganda while the government had nonetheless allowed it to take place in Bunyoro and Toro. To add to the complexities, by having intervened prior to the Constituent Assembly having had a chance to even consider the matter, the president henceforth also became the chief target of numerous petitions and protests pro and con restoration.

The pattern of confrontation and debate that subsequently ensued until virtually the present time became strongly polarised, with the NCT trying to mobilise public and political opinion in favour of restoration, and the Banyankore Cultural Foundation (BCF) determined to oppose it. The NCT, which at its foundation had given the impression that it intended to work towards a broader cultural agenda, increasingly concentrated its attention and mobilising efforts on the specific issue of kingship, in effect equating Ankole culture with kingship. As one strong restoration proponent, Maj. Gen. Salim Saleh, put it, there is 'dire need for the restoration of Obugabe because the culture of the Banyankore [is] dying fast owing to lack of a cultural leader' (*New Vision*, 31 January 2000).

One result of this narrowing of focus to the kingship issue on the part of the NCT was the alienation of some of its original membership, which at the time had joined expecting it to address a wider platform of interests (*New Vision*, 13 March 2000). Another effect was, predictably, to prompt the rival body supposedly similarly concerned with Ankole culture, though opposed to restoration, the BCF, likewise into alert and action. In fact, both organisations had been devoting most of their time on the Obugabe issue, pro and con, and, except for the establishment of a Runyankore school by the BCF in Kampala, have spent little energy on other aspects of the promotion of Ankole culture. Thus, at the threshold of the new millennium, the two groups were identified in the press as the 'pro-Omugabe' and 'anti-Omugabe' camps respectively, and hardly a statement was issued on the matter on behalf of the one without an instant rejoinder from the other.

Significantly, though, after a one-time effort in 1998 to reach an agreement in a joint meeting between the two groups had failed, this 'dialogue' never again became a direct one. Rather, it was conducted indirectly, through statements to the press or representations made to the government, which would subsequently be reported in the press. Any of these would in turn be criticised, denied or debated by spokespeople for the other group. In this connection, no matter how much both organisations ostensibly had 'culture' as their central concern and brief – and presumably even largely the same culture it was difficult not to gain the impression that the dispute had become a highly political and politicised one. This quality seemed characteristic not just for the way the debate was being conducted, but also for the way the stakes concerned appeared to be perceived. Positions hardened rapidly and seemed to leave little room for compromise or reconciliation. Thus conceived in 'all or nothing' terms, the dispute became one in which both parties felt they had to 'win' at all costs. One question this raises is whether that pattern had strictly been necessary and unavoidable.

But the curious onlooker might well first ask whether it was 'culture' for its own sake, and opposed interpretations of what this might contain, which the two rival associations were so fiercely debating and fighting over with respect to the former Ankole kingdom and the prospects of it getting restored? If that were the case, it could safely be taken as an indication of a truly exceptional commitment to higher cultural and spiritual values on the part of both groups, rarely to be found in most other parts of Africa or Europe. While theoretically allowing for such exceptional dispositions to occur, it may be useful also to consider alternative explanations. 'Culture', or 'tradition' for that matter, can also be used as an argument to advance the claims for particular positions, and privileges, of certain sections within a society over and against those of others. What matters then is what the presentation of the culture in question seems to suggest or imply as to where the dividing lines are to be drawn, and how that particular 'culture' can be put forward as demanding recognition of certain claims or differential allocation of social prestige and power.

In Ankole, it is such competitive claims as to what the specific 'culture' would contain that appear to be centrally at stake. But it is well to remember that the discourse on 'culture' that emerged in Uganda in connection with the restoration of the monarchies was a direct result of the government's invention of the idea of cultural rather than political kingdoms to justify restoration and allay the fears of opponents.[5] The essentially political debate on the restoration issue in Ankole thus got couched in ostensibly 'cultural' terms, to the extent that the two groups competing with one another over the issue have been consistently presenting themselves as 'cultural' organisations.

The final outcome of this competition, however, if it were to be resolved either one way or the other, in turn might be expected to add an aura of legitimacy to one or another way in which the local political system and process would be given further shape. Specifically, depending on what notion of 'culture' might in the end prevail, this could come to favour either a monarchy-centred patronage system of particular benefit to the 'traditionalist' Bahima elite (notably those with ties to the former Nkore) and a wider client retinue, or else a more egalitarian and open system in which entrepreneurial Banyankore of different rank and file would be likely to play prominent roles.

For a glimpse of what at least one aspect of restoration might come to mean concretely in Ankole, one now only needs to look at what has happened in neighbouring Toro and Bunyoro (and of course Buganda) since the reinstatement of the monarchies there: ministers and other office-holders have been appointed, claims on land and other properties re-tabled, new sources of revenue contemplated and installed, all to provide for the upkeep of new monarchy-oriented ministerial positions and support structures which are yet to demonstrate that they are socially relevant in developmental terms. In a still somewhat fluid situation within the Great Lakes region generally, in which the last word about state formation has not yet been said, it goes without saying that the stakes concerned are potentially very high and far-reaching.

The ostensibly 'political' quality and process characterising the Obugabe debate seemed to reflect a rather anomalous situation having arisen with respect to the handling of the issue. At the time of writing, the issue appears to have arrived at a stalemate hardly allowing new departures. Possibly the process could only have been given a different direction by higher political organs in the country, though in a way their hands were tied, too. One question in particular that had remained unclear arose from the fact that the constitution had not specified exactly how people's wishes were to be articulated, or to be represented and recorded, nor which body should decide about that. Adding to the complexity around this particular question, the NCT for its part has taken the position that reinstatement of the monarchy constituted such an intrinsic part of Ankole's culture that this could never be allowed to be put up for a public vote.[6] Among other things, this position seemed a rationalisation for the secret coronation which had been staged in 1993.

A variant to the proposal for a public vote, namely one in which the matter would be resolved in a collective vote by all LC-III and LC-V councillors and members of parliament of Ankole, had been proposed by First Deputy Premier Eriya Kategaya (himself from the region).[7] Even this met with strong resistance from the side of NCT, however. According to NCT's vice-chairman, George William Katatumba, this would 'amount to denying those Banyankore who adhere to a monarchical culture of their constitutional rights' (*The Monitor*, 16 February 2000). Evidently, therefore, this did not leave much space to arrive at an agreement even over basic procedures. Significantly, also, the statement appeared to reveal the NCT's position as being that even if only a section of the population would favour a return of the monarchy, that by itself would be sufficient for it to take place. That position, however, would seem just as problematic as the (hypothetical) suggestion that 99.99 per cent of the population concerned should have expressed themselves in favour before restoration can be considered.

The Uganda government for its part had all along taken the position that 'cultural' matters such as having traditional leaders were not its business ('as long as the people so wish'). Yet, whether it wanted this or not, by annulling Prince Barigye's coronation immediately after it took place in 1993, thus prior to the Constituent Assembly that was expected to deliberate on the matter, it had also placed itself into a position of final arbiter about the future of Ankole kingdom. Henceforth, therefore, its principle of 'neutrality' and 'non-involvement' could easily come to clash with its assumed arbiter role, and the two have indeed appeared to be in constant friction. At one level, the government was encouraging the two groups to try and sort out the question amongst themselves – which was about the last thing they would be able or prepared to do.

At another level, and in a situation where many people in regard to all kinds of issues are apt to ask first what the government's intentions are, there continued to be a fair amount of speculation that the government might be having its own agenda on the matter. People asked, for example, whether in his public campaigns for restoration, President Museveni's younger brother, Celeb Akandwanaho (more commonly known by his army nickname Salim Saleh), was merely exercising his constitutional right to hold a different opinion from that of the president, or whether he was letting up some trial balloons towards a final government position on the case?

Amidst all the noise and political heat to which the restoration issue gave rise in Ankole, it was striking to note that there was hardly any attention to the functions that the kingship, if restored, would perform. Significantly, beyond the general proposition of 'cultural leadership' expected of the Omugabe, arguments cast in favour of restoration did *not* point to essential social or cultural functions, carried over from historical times, remaining unfulfilled in the absence of kingship. This was in marked contrast to other parts of Africa, particularly West Africa, where *chiefdom* (somehow the vocabulary of 'kingship' never got introduced here) has retained a notable resilience until the present day.

In both francophone and anglophone West Africa, traditional chiefs continue to play significant roles as custodians of the land, in the settlement of disputes, as interpreters of customary law, in certain religious functions, as community representatives, and some other functions[8]. Some of these roles are controversial and contested, occasionally bringing the chiefs concerned into conflict with government officers or other stakeholders, yet no one would maintain that the offices concerned are 'empty' or devoid of societal functions. In the Ankole case this is different: largely as a result of the far-reaching extension and transformation of the institution during colonial times, it is no longer associated with any particular judicial, religious or other customary authoritative functions in the public mind. In this regard the absence of references to customary roles in the public debate about restoration is telling and significant. It underscores the fact that in the final analysis the debate is about the possible return of a neo-traditionalised institution, in which new ceremonial would substitute for customary functions.

A way out of the stalemate?

In the light of the continuing stalemate about the restoration issue in Ankole, the question arises whether it might not have been possible to conceive of less zero-sum kind of ways of handling a dispute of this kind. It could well be relevant to reflect on this question, if only to better appreciate the complexity of dimensions involved. By the same token, there could be at least a theoretical interest to explore whether at all there might still be any conceivable way out of the stalemate. Towards this end, a useful first step might be to consider the positions each of the key actors have been adopting in the dispute.

Starting with the Nkore Cultural Trust, it is of course perfectly reasonable and legitimate that an organisation has been brought to life that has set itself the goal of striving towards restoration of the Ankole kingship. After all, there had been a monarchy before, and if reinstatement depends on 'if the people so wish', it makes every sense for an interested 'civil society' organisation to take up this challenge and speak out in its favour. That is essentially what the NCT has done, even though it did not quite seem to 'let the people speak', but rather was couching its claims in terms of what Ankole 'culture' would demand. To the extent that the NCT articulates a position favoured by royalist circles in Ankole, it should not be surprising that it seems to be taking its cue from history rather than trying to articulate 'popular' demands. The historical part of its name, Nkore, points in that direction, while the notion of 'trust' evidently carries a conservationist connotation. But in taking up its role, it would also be reasonable to expect the NCT to appreciate the need to demonstrate that there would be broad public support for its agenda. One cannot just leave it at claiming the Obugabe back as a kind of natural right and expect the government to impose or approve it, while ignoring the (constitutionally based) call for a probing of popular sentiments and preferences. Besides, it would be important for the NCT, as for all other parties for that matter, to take cognisance of other prevailing views on the matter and consider their implications for one's own position.

As for the Banyankore Cultural Foundation, again, in what had essentially been a divided society it was entirely valid for an organisation like the BCF to have been founded in order to present an opposite and alternative agenda with regard to the question of Obugabe. As the first part of its name implies, it first of all sees itself as representing Banyankore, 'the people of Ankole'. If no other bodies seemed inclined to take account of broadly felt popular opinions about the matter in the first place, it was quite natural that a body like the BCF would seek to give voice to them. What remains significant, though, is the fact that in contrast to the NCT, which evidently was founded in order to advocate the concretising of a specific interest (and thus somehow felt less of a need to give voice to popular opinion as such), BCF's aim to try and prevent this from happening compelled it to serve as a vehicle for many amorphous feelings which in the end may be presumed to be converging indifference and opposition.

Still, while the points of departure of BCF and NCT are relatively clear, it is perhaps less clear what 'secondary' positions they should be adopting in the process. Since Ankole kingship is a historical fact, those for and against its restoration should make reciprocal concessions to recognise and respect the strong feelings of each other. In this connection, one of the insights which the original study for *Regalia Galore* had yielded was how much the Obugabe had historically been an institution of and for the Bahima in Nkore, and thus centrally important to them. This background would seem to deserve a certain recognition by all Banyankore alike, irrespective of whether or not in the end the monarchy were restored and in what particular way.

Likewise, the NCT for its part would need to recognise that reinstatement of a colonially restructured institution like that of Ankole kingship is by no means as self-evident as it might appear to them. In a way, one might say it is the tragic fate of the Obugabe to have become so much extended beyond its original domain that it has lost its proper historical foundation. As the original study of *Regalia Galore* revealed, the monarchy's incorporation into the colonial framework caused a once meaningful institution to become largely redundant. The extension of the formal jurisdiction of the Obugabe during colonial times could not but leave many or most Banyankore indifferent to it, and the most vocal parts of society even indignant about the premise of inequality it entailed. Given this background, it would be difficult to expect that the domain of a kingship which could once be extended by way of a colonial administrative measure would now be voluntarily and popularly accepted. The complexity of the case is such, therefore, that any attempt at resolution, in whatever way, would require mutual recognition of the concerns on the other side. 'Victory' thinking from either side would seem quite unproductive: rather, any concluding moment to all the deliberations on the issue should ideally come to figure as a high point in social and historical reconciliation (which in the end is worth more than 'winning' any social or ethnic battles).

As for the third party caught up in the complexity of the case, the Uganda government, in taking the formal position that 'kings' are 'cultural leaders' which therefore 'per definition' are not its business, it may actually have abandoned the room it could have used for a more active involvement. The government's position stemmed from its prior concern with the Buganda case, with regard to which its approach had been meant as a formula to keep the Kabaka out of politics.[9] However, 'political' here carries a different connotation, referring to engagement in day-to-day political processes. Deciding about having or not having kings within a larger state framework, even if it would concern a seemingly 'non-political' office, is surely a first order political matter deserving closest attention of a (republican) government.

With respect to the Ankole puzzle, one wonders whether a different government involvement might possibly have steered the issue away from deadlock, allowing a search for more creative solutions. In other, perhaps more bureaucratically inclined or endowed contexts, for example, one might have pursued alternative routes in trying to avoid having the issue being decided through competitive bargaining and campaigning. The latter tends to have the effect of polarising positions and may produce quite unpredictable outcomes. Instead, one might have opted, for example, for a 'committee scenario': installing a committee of enquiry charged by government with the task of looking into all aspects of the matter, or being given a specific brief and questions on the basis of which it is expected to conduct its investigations and make recommendations.[10] Such a committee would take its time, hear all parties concerned, and eventually produce a report with its findings and recommendations.

Government in turn would discuss this and could formulate its own position on the matter, possibly in 'white paper' format. Such policy paper could form the basis for a more informed debate in parliament or whatever other appropriate context, followed by final decision-making. If this seems a tedious process, which it may well be, it is worth remembering that the whole process of enquiry, reflection and structured discussion about the issues involved is likely to have its own clarifying effects, whatever they may be. One positive aspect of this could be that at least there will be better and fuller information about all the relevant aspects before any final decisions are reached. A second would be that in this process one would have considered and tested all scope for flexibility to bring opposite positions closer together. With some luck, such a process and dialogue would also have its own reconciling and learning effects, which in the context of a society like that of Ankole might well be one of its most important long-term advantages.

Now, clearly, the composition of any such a committee of enquiry would be a matter of utmost importance. In the present, as yet entirely hypothetical case, it would stand to reason that both the NCT and the BCF would need to be adequately represented (while indirectly also giving a fair representation of the clan structure) and might together constitute the bulk of the committee's membership. Surely, their joint involvement in any such committee could provide for an alternative, possibly more meaningful dialogue about matters of common interest and concern than many of the present indirect exchanges via the press. In addition, some other, third party membership might be invited on the committee for their comparative expertise on particular aspects, or perhaps to facilitate the dialogue, though expressly not to tip the balance of opinion in favour of one position or another.

Guiding questions a committee of such a nature might be invited to concentrate on could run along any of the following, roughly parallel lines: Is there any 'need' to re-introduce kingship in Ankole? What role or purpose would it be expected to serve? Are there any conceivable pre-conditions under which the restoration of kingship might become considered as a feasible option in Ankole society? Under what conditions, if any, could the re-introduction of Obugabe come to look acceptable to the vast majority of Ankole society? What kind of restructuring of the institution of kingship would be required to make it acceptable and welcomed by the population as a whole? Or, from an even more positively constructive interest and point of departure: Could the institution of kingship in Ankole be (re-)constituted in any conceivable way such that it might become a socially integrative force, overcoming rather than deepening ethnic divisions and animosities?

There could be numerous other possible questions, but the important point would be that they should allow and facilitate a joint search for possible pre-conditions. At the present stage and impasse of the debate in Ankole, it might be reasonable to raise questions such as the present ones. They would allow for either affirmative or negative answers, but in both cases the discussion would be furthered by a fair amount of background thinking and preparation. In a society in which some would feel that it needed an instrument like kingship as an integrative element, one should in principle expect flexible and serious efforts to come up with appropriate solutions, that is, an institution that could be expected to play such a role. If, finally, the issue would nonetheless come to a dead end, which of course remains a real possibility, at least one could say it has not been for lack of careful consideration.

Incidentally, it will be appreciated that these kinds of questions themselves depart from an understanding of institutions of kingship in which their format and constitution are not necessarily 'fixed', but are essentially flexible and adjustable, within limits, to new conditions and demands. There is nothing particularly unusual about this. It is consistent with historical practice and precedent in the case of various European monarchies, which at various times have been subject to major redefinition of their role and prerogatives. In several cases, the public debate and policy dialogue about the position of Western European royalty continues until today, often including the question of continuation, in adapted form, or termination and replacement by non-monarchical, republican representative institutions. In these debates, the underlying idea is that monarchism, in the final analysis is, an outdated edifice no longer befitting the requirements of the twenty-first century, though in the countries that still have it its role is continuously being adapted to changing circumstances and demands.

Far-reaching adaptation has also already been the experience of the Ankole monarchy itself. As the earlier parts of the present study have shown, during the twentieth century the institution of Ankole kingship has been drastically redefined in a number of respects, so much so that any contemplating of the institution's restructuring at the present time would in no way present a novelty. But if one were to take the position (either in propagating or opposing restoration) that there is no alternative for the institution's format than the one that 'exists', or rather, existed, i.e. the pre-1966 institution, then further exploration of alternatives, if any, will make little sense.

At the present point, it is of course quite uncertain that either the NCT or the BCF or both would be prepared to join in any such dialogue, even if there were prior agreement that the outcome would remain entirely open and contingent upon full consensus. The differences in their respective points of departure might be just too vast. Quite possibly, therefore, this would be 'a bridge too far', though it would nonetheless be interesting, and clarifying in a way, to see how each of the two organisations might respond to a proposition of this kind. At the same time, the sheer existence of two rival bodies both ostensibly committed to the furtherance of Ankole culture, but presumably having quite contrasted ideas as to what this should entail, appears indicative of serious rifts having re-emerged within the society and especially among its culturally most vocal segments. Hence, if the organisational expression of these rifts in the presence of the NCT and BCF may at first seem anomalous, it will be important to realise that the underlying social divisions which have re-surfaced in connection with the kingship issue in Ankole constitute the really serious matter in need of attention. Put again in briefest possible form, it is not so much kingship as such but the historical legacy and memory (and hence the future) of Bahima-Bairu relations which appear to be at issue in Ankole, at least to this outside observer. Clearly, it would seem in everybody's interest not to allow these to deteriorate, but to try and open a new chapter of cooperation, like what happened in the early days of the National Resistance Movement in Ankole.

It is precisely in this current impasse that seems reflective of this sociopolitical rift that other initiatives are conceivable which, even though not directly addressed to the question of kingship, might help reconcile rather than divide, and might even be more readily manageable. In the light of the very different understandings and experiences of history and culture in the Ankole region which are likely to be found within the NCT and the BCF, for example, it might be worth envisaging the possibility of a joint history project set up by the two organisations. Such a venture might be extremely helpful in determining the common ground as well as the major differences in their respective readings of history and historical relationships between the various ethnic communities in Ankole.

Again, while it may seem far-fetched at this moment to see the two bodies undertake such a joint project, consider the potential interest and pay-offs: a joint history project could, first of all, be an important learning exercise to all parties concerned. If one saw oneself jointly responsible in a venture to produce, say, an authoritative history of Ankole, then by the very nature of it such an exercise would call for profound and extensive dialogue between participants over the key forces that have been shaping Ankole society into its present form. One would not normally or necessarily expect this to 'resolve' various disputes, but at least to clarify them and produce better understandings of what significance others have been attaching to the same features or experiences manifested in a common context. But there must also be elements in common which it might be worth recognising as such and making explicit.

Taking this a few steps further, a joint history project for Ankole could extend into various different directions, and actually become quite an exciting project to take part in. For instance, it might look into common elements of clan structure, language, and customs for Bairu and Bahima and see where they differ and vary and where they meet. In the past, many such studies were undertaken separately for Bahima in particular but some also for Bairu, underlining difference and exclusiveness. Possibly, any such joint enquiry might be undertaken in the spirit of, or to promote, a kind of 'historic compromise'. After all, if there were greater preparedness to consider and acknowledge what one has 'in common', parties might also more readily accept and acknowledge what is 'different': either about the other group's background and involvement or about the latter's perception of history and their role in it. 'Learning from each other's history' could constitute a lead theme in any such exercise.

If any possible joint history project were to unfold, then at some point it might come to surveying the kingship situation prior to colonisation: Mpororo, Buhweju, Buzimba, Igara, Nkore, etc., mapping out the distinctiveness and similarities of each of these entities. The implication could be to show that until the end of the nineteenth century there had been a range of kingships, all of which could potentially be restored if there were an idea to restore pre-colonial kingship. Among other things, the project could then verify the possible claims to recognition of the dynasties of the Beenemafundo, the Beenekirenzi, the Benekihondwa, the Beeneruzira and the Beenerukari, among others, some of whose successors are to be found in the present Ntungamo district as well as some areas of Mbarara and Sembabule districts, (Cf. Morris,1962:20). Besides, a joint history project could possibly provide the proper context for examining the claims that, as an institution, the Ankole kingship is some 600 years old. As suggested above, if the idea is to restore the colonially restructured kingship, it might need to be recognised that its lifetime has extended just over 60 years. At any rate, the kingship experience in the region, from ancient times until its abrogation, would naturally constitute an extremely important aspect for any joint history enquiry to delve into.

Again, the role of a joint history project would not necessarily be to make recommendations about any future restoration of kingship. But if such a project were to devote attention to the issue, which of course it might well do, it could well come up with a conclusion that several pre-1900 entities would have valid theoretical claims to restoration. This might lead to proposals either to a) recognise them all; b) install a rotational 'chief among chiefs', like at one time in Busoga or in faraway Malaysia; or c) just let the matter rest. If, on the other hand, one wanted to hold on to the idea of restoring the extended post-1900 institution of Ankole kingship (on the premise that the presence of kings had once again become established as a norm in Uganda after 1993), then one should in principle accept the need for major structural adaptations which would make the institution acceptable to Ankole's population as a whole. A restructured, integrative institution of kingship with which all Banyankore could ideologically identify, for example, not unlike the way Buganda's Kabaka can in principle be seen to relate to all Kiganda clans, would potentially be an asset to Ankole in overcoming historic ethnic divisions. In particular, this would seem to call for reconsideration of the mode of inheritance and succession, such that in principle one could see Abagabe marry from any of the clans in Ankole, Bahima or Bairu, and thus produce descendants and heirs who might rightly consider themselves 'all-Ankole'. Again, however, it seems far from certain that those in favour of bringing back kingship to Ankole would be prepared to make that concession.

In this connection, while it is somewhat surprising that this particular aspect has not been taken up in the public debate, it should be noted that the pre-colonial Nkore kingship was not a hereditary institution. To be sure, historically contenders for succession would come from the Bahinda clan as a matter of course in Nkore, but among them there would typically be a struggle for power at the death of an Omugabe.¹¹ The idea of inheritance was only introduced during colonial times, and began with Gasyonga succeeding Kahaya. But if the pre-1900 institution were taken as the point of departure, an appropriate present-day equivalent for its particular mode of succession could simply be election from a slate of candidates who theoretically might come from any of the clans. At present, such an option may not exist: it remains to be seen whether those in favour of monarchical restoration would be prepared to engage in as fundamental a rethink of the institution as it might require for it to become of relevance to the society as a whole. At the same time, it remains hard to see how minority kingship, supported in practice by a relatively small body of 'adherents of monarchical culture', in the current phrasing in Uganda, could at all be a viable solution. Realistically, the expectation that one must count on a continuing impasse on this score seems at least as likely as achieving any meaningful breakthrough.

Towards an Ankole museum of history and culture: A far-fetched proposition?

If ever there were anything like a joint history project in which BCF and NCT might participate, with a big leap of imagination one might see this as potentially providing a platform for an even more ambitious undertaking. One truly challenging task that might be taken up within an ongoing history project could be to engage in the building of a museum of Ankole history and culture. Such a museum might serve many purposes, not the least of which would be to provide a concrete object for the ongoing dialogue and collaboration between BCF and NCT it would entail. Educationally, too, the creation of an imaginative museum would be of major value to the school system in Ankole and beyond. Above all, there is a rich culture and historical legacy in the Ankole region, which is well worth preserving and displaying for the benefit of all Banyankore as well as of visitors to the region.

Traditional Bahima livelihood patterns, for example, in more than one way are unique within the wider East African context, subject as they now are to drastic transformation and facing eventual disappearance. It would be extremely important to document all this and preserve it for posterity. Similarly, various aspects of traditional Bairu life and culture would warrant documentation and representation within the context of a museum, and could be engagingly displayed with various advanced techniques now available for such purposes.

Again, for many reasons, though above all as a focal point for people locally with an interest in the region's historical background, there could be untold benefits from the establishment of an Ankole museum of history and culture. Last but not least, the background and history of Ankole's kingship should naturally be given ample attention and prominence within a museum of this kind. Royalty everywhere brings with it numerous records and attributes that will attract public interest, and which can be complemented by relevant collections of photographs, film and video. The museum might also provide a fitting environment to accommodate Bagyendanwa, the Nkore royal drums, on its premises, together perhaps with other royal drums like Mashaija from Buhweju and Bitunta from Buzimba.

Clearly, therefore, there would in principle be a highly suitable project for joint action by the NCT and BCF, and a successful collaborative portrayal of Ankole culture in its manifold facets would in fact constitute a monument to the role of these organisations themselves. If successful, they might eventually even come to consider a merger. Still, history and culture by their very nature are subject to multiple and malleable interpretations, and this should certainly be expected in the present case. Clearly, in any joint activity like a shared museum project there would be numerous points on which BCF and NCT would need to compare notes and would want to register their agreement or disagreement with particular historical representations. Again, in as far as they would be able to resolve such issues, the pay-off would be a truly authoritative rendering of local history, in turn with substantial positive effects on socio-ethnic relations. But even if no consensus were reached on various key aspects, which given the background history should not be too surprising, a joint museum project could still make sense. It could allow each of the two organisations to concentrate its attention on the aspects and items it considered of primary importance from its own perspective, each working on a different floor, for example. If this involved matters invoking contrasted interpretations, a museum that would thus accommodate different perspectives on vital matters of common interest and history might still be considered a unique venture, or in fact even more so.

Conclusion: A review of 'options'

In the light of the above discussion, it is not quite accidental that a fresh edition of a book on the history and background of Ankole kingship should have ended on a proposal for a museum project on Ankole's history and culture. It seems clear from all accounts that there is an extremely interesting story to be told and re-told in connection with Ankole's kingship and its place in history and culture. A proper museum would seem to be the proper place for this. It could place Ankole's kingship in its specific historical and cultural context, and it could present that context itself with all the richness and different points of interest for which it has rightly been drawing attention. Besides, a museum project, connected to an ongoing forum over the nature and contents of Ankole culture, might possibly help to attenuate some of the social divisions which in an indirect way the institution of kingship had been giving rise to.

When contemplating possible ways of tackling the Ankole kingship issue, a museum project as suggested here might itself be taken as one possible option, with potentially beneficial effects in terms of social reconciliation and integration among Ankole's population groups. Certainly, this option deserves serious attention. Other options, as touched upon in the text above, would go in very different directions, and would each be likely to generate very different kinds of effects and political repercussions. When recapitulating these in conclusion, therefore, several of these may theoretically be noted as an 'option', though hardly being recommendable if one's aim is a peaceful exit out of the current deadlock, while others may, to different degrees, be more realistic or feasible. In trying to identify these variations, it will be useful also to see which 'option' is likely to get the support of which population and political segments within Ankole society.

The first of these 'options' would be the NCT's present line, namely, to strive for the restoration of Ankole kingship but keep this focused on the Nkore-originated institution, thus with a Bahinda-based royal dynasty as it was before it was terminated in 1967. This would represent the most direct form of restoration of what there was immediately before, i.e. the colonially created institution, but also the one most likely to provoke strong reactions and deepening social conflict, which on that ground seems ill-advisable. This option would draw its main support from the circles now engaged with the NCT, that is, various individuals (Bahima and Bairu) who had a role in the former Ankole kingdom structure, others who might aspire to similar positions within a restored framework, in addition to members of the Bahinda elite who would regard themselves as having a historical claim on the kingship, several high-ranking army officers among them. It is important to note that this option would not be able to count on general Bahima support. Many Bahima, especially those from historical regions other than Nkore, would seem disinclined to lend their support to the restoration of the 'colonial' monarchical institution.

A second 'option' would be derived from the first one, except for one radical departure: this would seek to emulate the 'Buganda-model' and entail an opening up of the lines of inheritance and succession, thus expecting the Abagabe not only in theory but also in practice to marry from any of the other Ankole clans. If it could materialise, this option would be likely to score rather high in terms of prospects for social integration of Bahinda, Bahima and Bairu in Ankole, and might thus count on fairly broad popular support. However, the problem with this option is of course that it has been available all the time, but that the kings and princes concerned have never seemed much inclined to give it serious consideration. The problem reflects an even much broader issue: Bahima-Bairu intermarriage generally remaining extremely rare, a royal initiative in this respect would constitute more than a novelty and offer a truly unprecedented role model, – virtually a 'revolution from above'. As things stand, though, even if it would represent the difference between having a kingship or not, this route just does not seem realistic. Lack of flexibility on this point among the (non) -'ruling' Bahinda might seem to call for more serious consideration on their part of various alternative 'options'.

A third option would be the restoration not just of the Nkore monarchy, but also of the kingships of Buhweju and Buzimba (in present-day Ibanda) as well as the break-away kinglets in Igara, Shema, and Ntungamo that had split off from the former Mpororo kingdom. This might take away the apprehensions and reservations about restoration among members of the royal clans of some of the other kingships incorporated into the colonial Ankole kingdom. By implication, the territorial domain of each of these (as well as of Nkore) would remain limited to that of the respective historical entities, and would not include non-kingdom areas such as Bunyaruguru. This option therefore might represent the most accurate historical reconstruction of institutions of kingship, and to some degree diminish though not eliminate the ethnic issue. Practically, though, it would entail a certain amount of fragmentation, and it would by no means be certain whether all the respective royal lineages would actually be interested in taking part in any such venture. While figuring fairly prominently as an argument against the restoration of the Nkore kingship by itself, this option seems unlikely to elicit much broadened support even among Bahima.

A fourth option would be a further variant of this, namely to consider some form of a rotating *primus inter pares* role among these various kings and kinglets, roughly along the lines as once existed in Busoga. It would still give Ankole a kind of monarchical status, presumably with a somewhat extended range of support from the various ex-kingdoms that were once incorporated into Ankole, such as Buhweju, Igara and the various split-offs from Mpororo. It could be argued that it would be relatively more cost-effective than the third option, and to some extent constitute an antidote to potential fragmentation. It would amount to a somewhat complex arrangement, but theoretically it could be done. However, even if it might be able to count on a widened area of Bahima support as compared to the 'Nkore' option, it remains unlikely to generate broad Bairu support and in that regard would still appear a basically non-viable proposition.

A fifth possibility among the range of options would be that of an elective kingship, theoretically with candidates from any of the clans within the Ankole region. In a way this would constitute the most radical as well as the most democratic form of reforming the kingship. However, it needs emphasising that historically it would by no means be without equivalent and precedent: as noted above, in pre-colonial Nkore and Mpororo succession took place not on a hereditary principle but on the basis of competition between different (Bahinda) contenders. Hereditary succession came only as part of the colonial invention. Extending the historical practice and privilege of competition to all the clans in a sense would appear only a relatively small step, constitutionally speaking, and might constitute one way of overcoming the ethnic divide which is now re-surfacing. Competition as such could take place with the means available in the twenty-first century rather than those of the nineteenth, i.e., by ballot box rather than spears. The principle would nonetheless remain the same. This alternative is likely to receive fairly substantial support among Bairu (and possibly from some of the Bahima who would like to see the end of ethnic distinctions being made), though it is uncertain whether they would prefer this option instead of having no restoration of kingship whatsoever and just letting the matter rest. At the same time, whether the monarchist sections of the Bahinda elite and others allied with them would be positively disposed towards accepting this option in order to allow consideration of a more generalised kingship, may remain a big question. But then the question might well be asked whether they can be considered to 'own' the kingship and, if so, whether that can or should still be sustained in the twenty-first century. After all, the issue concerns much more than the question of kingship *per se*, and kingship or whatever other form of government might in the first instance be seen as an expression of how a society has chosen to organise and govern itself.

Fairly close still to the option of an elective kingship, along the lines of clan-based competition, would be the idea of a different kind of representative ceremonial function as a sixth option. Again, recruitment could be envisaged by either direct or indirect election, the key difference being that in this case the function concerned should no longer be considered as a form of kingship. Instead, non-royal ceremonial office holders chosen by election would rather be and function like the constitutional heads that were installed in various districts shortly after Uganda's independence. In the neighbouring Kigezi district, for example, which had no tradition of kings, such a head, titled *Rutakirwa*, was installed and for some years proved quite a popular innovation. Again, this option would be more open, democratic, and 'republican' than most others before and might appeal to larger sections of the population, especially Bairu. The main question it would leave unanswered is whether or to what extent Ankole society at the present time 'needs' a ceremonial office of this kind, and whether it would be prepared to absorb the costs of its upkeep.

Epilogue: Regalia Galore Revisited   125

The seventh and final option, then, would represent one possible answer to this last question, by simply favouring no change from the current status quo. Though probably implying a further prolongation of the stalemate about the restoration issue with the NCT and BCF as the main contenders for at least some time to come, under the circumstances this may well represent the most realistic option, as well as the most likely one to occur. Again, there seems little doubt that this option would be the preferred one amongst many Bairu, especially among educated and entrepreneurial categories. Still, one should not assume that all Bahima would be opposed to it: not a few would rather see no change from the present situation than have the prospect of continuing social conflict about the restoration of a disputed kingship.

Leaving the matter to rest where it stands would seem to be in broad accordance with the lukewarm reactions observed at the time of the monarchy's abolition in 1967, described earlier in this book. The apparent indifference at the time seemed to reflect the loss of a once meaningful role which the monarchy had incurred due to its insertion as part of the colonial institutional framework, as well as the fact that the kingship remained far removed from the concerns and preoccupations of the vast majority of Ankole's population. The Bairu saying, 'It does not matter who takes over, they are all kings', seemed expressive of that distance and the indifference it generated. That indifference still seems there among large parts of the population, though due to the distance just alluded to it might, when pressed, be more likely to turn into opposition than accommodation. It is striking to note that in the debate thus far over the kingship issue, this basic indifference and silence among the majority of the population has never received a response. Against the background of the Ankole monarchy's loss of institutional and symbolic relevance in the twentieth century, it is noteworthy that questions like why would one want to have a kingship again in the first place, what would it have to offer, and what would a prospective monarch be expected to do, have just not been taken up.

If the kingship issue in Ankole is unlikely to be brought to an end that might satisfy all interested parties, it would still seem better to approach the matter in a positive way instead of just leaving it at that. The proposal for a museum of Ankole culture and history as suggested above, though not presented here as one of the 'options', might possibly constitute the preferred action from the perspective of more than one of the contending parties at the present time. Perhaps it should be given a try.

In conclusion, we might note that in recent years, against the backdrop of failed or failing systems of governance in various parts of post-colonial Africa, there has been a wave of propositions calling for attention to a 'betting on tradition' as an alternative in different regions of the continent. The underlying idea of these propositions is that the familiarity and feelings of security which would be associated with traditional institutions like kingship or chiefship might provide a closer fit with prevailing cultural values and allow better chances for culturally specific paths of governance and development. When considering any such culturally 'authentic' alternatives for possible adoption, however, parties concerned will do well to critically examine the powers and interests in support of the tabling of alternative propositions for governance in terms of 'tradition' and 'culture' arguments. Also, the particular 'tradition' claimed may itself warrant some probing: not a few supposedly 'traditional' institutions had basically lost their former glory and meaning due to their redefinition and incorporation into colonial structures, as the original study for *Regalia Galore* had found to be true for Ankole's kingship. Instead, new claims may be laid for privileged access to public resources, power and esteem, all in the name of 'tradition' as a seemingly higher purpose and legitimisation, though actually representing the interests of only a very specific segment of the community concerned. Chances then are of serious social conflict rather than reconciliation being generated by such re-traditionalisation. Ankole could become one such case, precisely if priority is not given to improving community social relationships.

Notes

1   Incidentally, the drafters of the (Republican) constitution made it a point to refer to the 'institution of traditional or cultural leaders' rather than to 'kingship'; only a subsequent clarification spells out that 'traditional leader or cultural leader' means a king or similar traditional leader or cultural leader by whatever name called' (Ch. 16, Art. 246 (5))
2   According to a statement from the Nkore Cultural Trust (NCT), the organisation actively engaged in propagating re-instatement of the Ankole monarchy, the NCT would propose to shelve the issue till 2003 so as to avoid their campaigning on the issue getting mixed up with that for presidential and parliamentary elections (*New Vision*, 15 March, 2000). As the NCT attached several conditions to this proposal, which it may prove difficult to fulfill, including the demand that the Uganda government now first recognises the heir designate to the throne as 'Prince' and should return 'his' property to him, it seems likely that the dispute will last for some more time to come.
3   Interview with James Kahigiriza, NCT chairman, *New Vision*, 15 March 2000. It might be noted, though, that even in respect of Nkore there was an inclination among informants interviewed by Roscoe in the early part of the twentieth century to provide him each time with more extended genealogies of former Abagabe, presumably out of an interest to emulate Buganda. See John Roscoe, *The Banyankole*, Cambridge, 1923:34.
4   I am indebted for this point to the Rev. Bishop Y. Bamunoba.
5   I am grateful to Justus Mugaju for drawing my attention to this point.
6   Such a position might not have been shared by Queen Elizabeth of England, who had made it known that she would not object to the Australian plebiscite organised in 1999 to decide whether Australia should become a republic or remain under the British monarchy.

Epilogue: Regalia Galore Revisited

7   Actually, there had already been a meeting of all LC-V councillors from the three Ankole districts at the president's home in 1993, where all but one voted against reinstatement.
8   This has been usefully examined in E. Adriaan B. van Rouveroy van Nieuwaal, *L'Ètat en Afrique face àla chefferie: Le cas du Togo*, Paris/Leiden: Karthala-ASC, 2000.
9   That objective was hardly reached: the Buganda government is now being reconstituted, with ministers being appointed for various portfolios, all under the guise of the 'cultural leader' principle. The process is reminiscent of the negotiations that took place in preparation for Uganda's independence in 1962, when especially a strong lobby on behalf of Buganda, commonly identified as the Mengo establishment, submitted claims for autonomous structures and offices based on arguments of 'tradition'. Only a few years later, the 'tradition' discourse made place for one highlighting ethnic confrontation.
10 The Constitutional Commission had already played a role that included some such elements. However, following the Kabaka's re-installation, it could be argued that a new situation had come into being in Ankole which might best be approached through a specifically tailored committee framework.
11 See page 17 above for a discussion with the former Omugabe and senior princes on this question.

Appendix I

Memorandum by the Elders of Ankole to the President, General Idi Amin Dada on the Restoration of Kingdoms[1]

We the representatives of the Elders of Ankole gathered in Mbarara on Monday 23rd August, 1971 wish to congratulate Your Excellency and the men of the Uganda Armed Forces on the successful take-over of Government on 25th January, 1971, and also on the manner in which Your Excellency has conducted the affairs of this country since you assumed its leadership as President of the Second Republic of Uganda.

The people of Ankole, and indeed the whole of Uganda look forward to your continued leadership so that this country may take its proper place among other progressive and peaceful nations of the world. Your Excellency, permit us also to take this opportunity on behalf of the people of Ankole to thank you for the honour you did us and the love you showed us by visiting our District only a few days ago. Your visit which had been long and anxiously awaited was hailed by thousands of people in Ankole as it enabled you to see for yourself the undoubted support that Your Excellency commands in the District.

Your Excellency, during your visit you talked to the people in the language they understand, you listened to their problems and requests with all your patience and you brought them nearer to you than any other leader has ever done. For this and for many other things you have done, we thank you most sincerely.

Your Excellency, may we thank you also for the good will you have shown towards the former rulers of this country since the Military take-over of Government – the return of the remains of the late Sir Edward Mutesa, the honour and respect which you and your Government paid at the funeral of the late Sir Tito Winyi, the restoration of property to Prince Kaboyo and the assistance you have continued to render to Sir Charles Gasyonga.

Your Excellency, the Elders of Ankole feel that this is a period when your Government is busily engaged in the programme of reconstruction and re-organisation of the affairs of the Nation; a period when no energies and efforts should be lost in building Uganda as a strong united country and also a period when all of us living in Uganda must look forward and not backwards.

Your Excellency, the Elders of Ankole feel that while there may be merit in re-examining some of the past deeds of the former President Milton Obote and his Government, your Government should not be rushed into taking decisions on matters which may distract your attention from, and frustrate your efforts in Nation building.

Your Excellency, in our view, the question concerning the restoration of Kingdoms is one of those crucial matters which we feel should not be raised or even discussed in the Second Republic of Uganda, because of the following reasons :

(a) It is your declared Policy that all political activities are suspended at the present time. The restoration of Kingdoms would most likely revive political divisions and factionalism contrary to the declared policy of Government. It is our view that if Uganda is to develop as a strong United Sovereign Nation, any divisive tendencies must not be allowed to emerge.

(b) The country at the moment faces a very heavy deficit, the country's financial position cannot therefore sustain any expenditure connected with the restoration of Kingdoms. In addition Kingship imposes all sorts of indirect taxations, all of which are undesirable.

(c) Present circumstances demand that all our efforts and resources in the Second Republic of Uganda should be concentrated on the economic and social reforms of the country for the benefit of many, instead of being used to enhance the prestige of a few individuals.

(d) The people in Kingdoms Districts have in the past shown a tendency of divided loyalty between their former Rulers and the Central Government. For the Military Government to consolidate its position and to carry out its programme of re-organisation unimpeded a situation which tends to create divided loyalty among the people must be avoided at all costs.

(e) The 18 points declared by the soldiers on the take-over of Government included the statement that Uganda will continue to be a Republic. This was further repeated at the State House, Entebbe, where the representatives of the Royal families were present. It would be going back on the soldiers' word if we started talking about the restoration of Kingdoms. Government must not give in to pressures of this kind.

Your Excellency, we say these things not with any malice, but we strongly feel that if we are to march forward to our stated goal of freedom and progress we must break with the past where this stands in our way and therefore our views must be accepted in this spirit.

In conclusion Your Excellency, we reiterate on behalf of the people of Ankole our full support to you and your Government. The people of Ankole are behind you in what you are doing and have every confidence that you will successfully accomplish the great task that you have set out to do for God and our Country.

The memorandum was signed by the following people: Z. C. K. Mungonya (Chairman); B. K. Bataringaya (Secretary); Canon Y. Buningwire (Member); P. K. Garubungo (Member); E. C. Cook (Member); C. B. Katiti (Member); A. Mulumba (Member); Y. Makaru (Member); W. Mukaira (Member); E. T. Kihika (Member); T. K. Kururagire (Member); N. K. Bananuka (Member); Sheik A. Kadunyu (Member); Haji Abbas Kayemba (Member); E. Rutehenda (Member) and J. B. K. Bwerere (Member).

Note

1 Source: *Uganda News*, Ministry of Information and Broadcasting, Kampala, Uganda, 24 August 1971.

Appendix II

Memorandum by the Elders of Buganda to the President, General Idi Amin Dada, on the Restoration of Kingdoms[1]

We, some of the Elders (Abataka) in Buganda, beg the honour to address Your Excellency over the very important issue being spoken about, almost in a propaganda form, particularly in our two English Daily papers, over the Radio and UTV, against the restoration of Kingship in Buganda.

When the Baganda Elders met you at the International Conference Centre on 5th August, 1971, you explained that to create a nation in which every citizen would be free and happy, was your cardinal aim; that the Military Government wanted to foster a spirit of love between all citizens of Uganda and to do away from the hearts of Ugandans the constant worry and fear that Mr. Obote had made his administrative tools and that you wanted to destroy the divide and rule policy which Mr. Obote and his General Service practised very well in order to perpetuate their stay in Government.

But from what we have read in the press and heard over our radio and TV sets, we have come to wonder, Your Excellency, whether it will be easy to effect the ideals you outlined to us at the Conference Centre, when, as it seems, once again, the rest of the nation has been allowed to stand up and shout us down, and shut us up.

This is why we are prompted to let you know that ever since our Independence Day in 1962, Buganda had never known what Independence is, until you liberated us on 25th January, 1971. This is why we went wild with joy and jubilation. Below, we list some of the reasons why since 1962 Buganda has existed in the most unhappy mood.

(1) Immediately after our independence celebrations, 1962, Obote, his General Service and henchmen started inciting hatred between the Baganda and the Banyoro over the issue of the lost counties (DIVIDE AND RULE).

(2) In 1964, at Nakulabye, Obote killed a number of our people some of whom were tender children.

(3) During the very same period Obote killed more of our children at Bulange, Mengo.

(4) We were shocked by the death of our children of St. Mary's Kisubi; we were more shocked, though, by the manner in which they died and the way Mr. Obote behaved towards a bereaved nation. (He never uttered a single word of sympathy; not even to the unlucky parents of the dead children).

(5) Obote, acting on his own, withdrew the Uganda Constitution of 1962, a contract that had been agreed upon by all Ugandans.

(6) Without any justifiable cause, Obote attacked the Kabaka's Palace at Mengo, May 23rd, 1966, killing hundreds of innocent people and forcing the late King Sir Edward Mutesa II into exile, where Obote was blood-thirsty enough 'to go' and kill him. Besides, it has been proved beyond doubt that Obote killed Daudi Ocheng, an M.P. from Buganda.

On 24 May 1966, Obote declared a state of emergency in Buganda, imprisoned the Late Kabaka's wife, Lady Damali, princes and princesses, and very many other prominent Baganda. He declared defunct the Buganda Lukiiko and abolished our Kingship.

During this time, he ruled us as if we were his slaves; he tortured us without pity and concern, and made us suffer constant ulcers from misery, worry and fear. Many Baganda businessmen were refused licences. Their business got wasted and re-introduced the Colonial-like rule of the D.C.'s which had been abolished as far back as 1942 (sic).

When the Late King Mutesa II died, Obote climaxed his hatred for us. He ordered us not to mourn our dead King and used guns to disperse those who had gone to pray for the dead at Namirembe. For those who managed to go and attend the funeral rites in Britain were put in prisons on their return. At the same time, 1969, Obote imprisoned our most revered Prince Badru Kakungulu. and Princess Nnalinya Irene Ndagire. Your Excellency, from 1962 to 25th January, 1971, the Baganda were Obote's Slaves.

Ever since the Military take-over, yours has been a marvellous administration. You have gone to the people everywhere in the country. You have listened carefully to the requests of all Elders from different area of Uganda. When you met us at Conference Centre, we also told you of the most important thing we wanted : 'OUR KING', because Obote used force of the gun to abolish the Kingship. Yet we used peace and humbleness to request for the restoration of our Kingship.

Your Excellency, from what we have outlined above, you can destroy our Kingship; to oppress and enslave the Baganda. The suffering we witnessed, and the losses we endured, were all unique in that no other single area of Uganda can show the same scars as we can from the daily wounds Obote inflicted upon us.

As you already know, Your Excellency in order to commit all those atrocities, Obote was all the time being helped by his relative Akena Adoko, and other close friends like Mukombe-Mpambara and Basil Bataringaya. With the help of these men, Obote kept Buganda in a 5-year period of Emergency Regulations, and imprisoned more than 4,000 Baganda.

We implore you to understand fully that although Obote is in Tanzania, his people – Abasi Balinda, Lwamafa, Katiti, Karyegesa, Bikangaga, the NUSU boys and girls, his deep supporters from Lango and a few from Acholi, are here, and working hard to further Obote's plans and aims. They plan, they talk not with love for their fellow Ugandans, but in order to create a mess of things and if possible to see Obote back.

Surprisingly all these we have enumerated above are the very same people who lead delegations to you, Your Excellency, and claim to have right advice to give you about Kingship in Buganda. What will they talk to you except what Obote wants them to say? And, Your Excellency, we want to stress the fact to be careful of the NUSU organisation. Obote promised these young students Parliamentary Seats. By all means they will fight hard to see him back.

We beg to make another point very clear Your Excellency that when we request you for the restoration of Kingship in Buganda, we do not want that King to rule Uganda. The Baganda know better than that. We want a King for Buganda and Buganda alone. The money to run this Kingship will come from us Baganda. Was it the Kingship which messed up with 700,000,000/- from the Uganda's treasury? It was Republican Obote and his socialist friends, who used to curse the Kingship and yet managed to throw the country into such a debt.

We pray that Elders from other areas request to be granted things pertaining to their areas, but not to meddle about in the affairs of other elders. We pray that the apparent Campaigns on the Radio, UTV and in the press against what we the Elders in Buganda requested be checked a bit. Otherwise from the present trend of affairs, people like Mukombe-Mpambara, Bataringaya etc. are secretly rejoicing, why? Because they see their plans of Divide and Rule still being allowed to operate in Uganda. Our main fear is that in the end these Lango elders, the NUSU students may still think of destroying you, Your Excellency and our beloved Armed Forces, when they get the chance. We want freedom. But there is always a limit to excessive freedom. While we are busy sorting out what went wrong, too much freedom should be checked. The secret plan of Obote known men, is to see the Baganda turn and hate you. They sit with burning envy and hatred as they watch the way Baganda love you and follow you. They know the Baganda are behind you wholeheartedly. They plan to make you lose that overwhelming support you have in Buganda. This is why we humbly beseech you to be much more careful about their plans.

From 1894 to 1963, Uganda was a Republic with its head as the Governor or the Governor General. In that Republic we had the Abakama, the Omugabe, the Kyabazinga and the Kabaka. But we had districts without these such rulers. *And Uganda was happy and progressive.*

In 1963/66 Uganda became a full Republic with a President on top this time. Each area had its sub-head. Things where working out very very smoothly. But in 1967 without consulting with anybody, Obote created his own constitution and his own Dictatorial Republic, in which he, alone, elected everybody else in the administration of Uganda. We the elders of Buganda had no support for such a Government, because we fully believe in peaceful negotiation at a negotiating table. This is the only way, we believe, without emotions and hatred for one another that the affairs of the State can run smoothly.

Your Excellency, you have heard of the tribal problems in Zambia. These are not created by Kings. There are no Kings. They are created by greedy, self-seeking politicians. Alternatively, you know, for example, the King of Ashanti in Ghana was recently restored. Kings are peacefully helping President Gowon of Nigeria to run the State. Even in Spain, after more than 30 years the state has decided to go back to Kingship.

We think Uganda has two deeply rooted ways of looking at things: (i) There are the Baganda in Uganda, who immensely love their Kings; (ii) There are the rest of the Ugandans who immensely hate Kings.

In peaceful Uganda, Your Excellency, these two groups must honour one another and love one another. Even America (Capitalism) and Russia (Communism) sit at table and talk peacefully. Why can't we, we Ugandans of the same family. We who love our Kingship should not impose this idea on others. But those who do not like Kingship should not simply impose this idea on us. There must be mutual respect and understanding.

We always kneel down and pray for you, Your Excellency. We pray that the God who enabled you to release us from Obote's chains, may also enable you to put right all that went wrong.

Note

1 Source: *Uganda News,* Ministry of Information and Broadcasting, Kampala, Uganda, 24 August 1971.

Appendix III

Memorandum by the Elders of Kigezi to the President, General Idi Amin Dada, on the Restoration of Kingdoms[1]

1. We, representing the elders of Kigezi District, assembled here in Kabale, on Tuesday, 17th August, 1971, wish to congratulate Your Excellency and your Government on the sound, practical and meaningful policies which Your Excellency's Government has so far initiated and implemented. The people of Kigezi, as Your Excellency are already aware, fully and unreservedly support Your Excellency and your Government.
2. Your Excellency, we the people of Kigezi have noted with full appreciation and satisfaction the emphasis which Your Excellency's Government has put on love, brotherhood, domestic tranquillity and national unity. We have noted how indeed Your Excellency's Government is fully committed to the service of this land and how it is a Government of Action. The people of Kigezi are also extremely pleased with your Government's policies and actions based on God and Truth. We know that any Government whose policies and actions are based on these criteria, like yours, is the only Government which can give its people the best possible service. Your Excellency, Kigezi is equally happy with your Government's determination to establish peace, harmony, freedom, and prosperity for the people of Uganda and their posterity. The people of Kigezi, therefore, are indescribably happy with your Government's sincerity, determination and commitment to establish a one truly united Uganda. We, in Kigezi, are equally determined and committed to support Your Excellency's Government's efforts in the achievement of these noble and nationalistic goals.
3. We, the people of Kigezi, have, however, noted with surprise and dissatisfaction the views expressed by some of our Brother Elders from Buganda Region during the Elders Conference which was recently held at the Conference Centre at which they requested the restoration of a Monarchy in Buganda. Their request would imply that the same restoration of Monarchs should be considered for other areas in this Republic where such institutions existed before. We wish to inform Your Excellency that this request which has been followed by representatives of elders in Buganda campaigning in the rest of the country to support the move, has caused widespread concern and indignation throughout Kigezi District. We also wish to inform Your Excellency that the people of Kigezi are so completely opposed to the restoration of these institutions that if they were restored, it would, in our view, be a retrogressive step. The people of Kigezi, therefore, wish to disassociate themselves completely from such an idea and move.
4. Your Excellency, the whole of Uganda hailed the very wise and highly nationalistic decision of the Officers, and Men of the Uganda Armed Forces as proclaimed on the 20th February, 1971, that Uganda would remain a Republic. Your Excellency, you yourself have repeatedly stated this decision, including the occasion when you addressed that particular conference of elders from Buganda Region. It is,

therefore, disheartening and distressing that some of our fellow citizens are trying to revive an issue which, in our opinion, has already been settled. We, the people of Kigezi, consider that there should be no further discussion on this matter. We feel that there are other National Issues of reconstruction, reconciliation and National development to embark upon rather than dealing with matters of history which are no longer of national benefit. People of Kigezi are aware that not all the elders at that Conference were of the view that the institution should be reinstated. We believed that those who share that view are mainly of the old order who hold rigid beliefs and particularly those who reaped from such institutions or see a ray of hope that should such institutions be restored they will stand to amass personal gain. We particularly believe that the progressive and forward looking people living in Buganda could not possibly find justification for the restoration of monarchs especially in the spirit of the Second Republic. It is therefore the strong view of the people of Kigezi that the Government of the Second Republic of Uganda should not at all entertain any possibility of reopening discussion on this issue and that the Government should therefore treat this matter completely as a dead issue. It is the view of the people of Kigezi that the decision to retain Uganda as a Republic is the most rational and in the best interests of the people of Uganda. The people of Kigezi are of the view that the Second Republic of Uganda should follow the policy of forwards ever and backwards never. It is in conformity with this desired view that the people of Kigezi would consider the restoration of any form of monarchy anywhere in Uganda as a most unfortunate step which would not only be repugnant in our present society but would definitely cause undesirable disunity in Uganda, and, as previously mentioned, hamper Uganda's economic and social development. We also are of the opinion that the restoration of this institution would lead to victimisation and possible bloodshed in the Region.

5. As Your Excellency and your Government and indeed, the whole of this Republic are aware, these tribal institutions were mainly responsible for the disunity of Uganda, as for example, when it was found necessary to institute federal states within the National State of Uganda. They were mainly responsible for tribal misunderstanding, mistrust and in some cases hatred that were prevalent in our society. They were mainly responsible for tribalism which existed before they were abolished. It is an indisputable fact that many of our people owed allegiance to tribal monarchs and their tribal governments more than they owed to Uganda and the Uganda Government. It is also a well known fact that many of our people preferred to be identified with their local monarchical institutions in preference to Uganda and its National Government. As a result of these institutions, tribalism had gone to such an extent as to completely frustrate any form of National Government whether federal or unitary. Some of these institutions considered their regional governments to be at par with the National Government. Kigezi believes that National interests must of necessity override local interests. Kigezi stands for and will always support Your Excellency and your Government's efforts to establish a truly united Uganda.

6. We, the people of Kigezi, believe that the existence of any institutions such as monarchs must be fully justified either socially or economically. We are aware that before the advent of the White Man, these institutions were essential and

justified because the monarchs and tribal and clan rulers were executive. People looked at them as their source of power, identification, security and inspiration. It will, however, be completely obvious even to the extreme monarchists that this age is gone and never to return. They also should agree that even if these institutions were revived, they would have very little to do as they would be non-executive whose main duties would be to perform the trivial tribal rites. It will be obvious even to those clamouring for the restoration of these institutions that these institutions would no longer perform such functions as appointments of chiefs, allocation of land, trial of cases which formerly included even sentencing offenders to death, defence of tribal areas and the like, as these have naturally and rightly been taken over by appropriate arms of the Uganda Government, which arms, we firmly believe, should not surrender them to local and tribal institutions. The re-establishment of these institutions will be unjustifiably expensive. If they were re-established, it would, in our view, mean setting up full tribal governments with all their monarchical paraphernalia. We are of the firm belief that even if this country had an inexhaustible source of finance, such money would be better spent on schemes which have the slightest touch of justification rather than on these luxurious and only prestigious institutions. We believe strongly that under no circumstances would such institutions be economically and even socially justified in modern Uganda. It is, in our view, therefore obvious that even if these institutions were justified, and of course they are no longer, this country is not economically in a position to accommodate them. It will be obvious that the restoration of a monarchy in Buganda cannot be considered in isolation. It will obviously and inevitably lead to similar requests by the former kingdom districts.

7. Your Excellency, we wish finally to state and re-affirm that we people in Kigezi are truly committed to the spirit and the letter of love, brotherhood and unity in this Republic. We strongly believe that restoration of any monarchy in Uganda would not be in the best interests of this country. We firmly believe that anything short of complete Unity in Uganda is unacceptable as it will hinder us in the fulfilment of our cherished goals. We feel it our duty and obligation, therefore, that we cannot keep quiet on an issue, although raised outside Kigezi, which will deter the harmonious development of our motherland. It is in this spirit that we have been prompted to address this memorandum to Your Excellency. We hope that our Brothers in Buganda Region and elsewhere will take our stand in the sincere spirit in which it has been made.

Note

1   Source: *Uganda News*, Ministry of Information and Broadcasting, Kampala, Uganda. 24 August 1971.

Bibliography

Agetereine. Runyankore paper, fortnightly, Mbarara.

Ankole Government and District Administration. Annual District Reports-Eishengyero minutes. Official correspondence and other archival materials. *Report of the Ankole Kingdom Customary Laws' Committee,* Mbarara, 1964.

Apter, David E. *The Political Kingdom in Uganda: A Study in Bureaucratic Nationalism,* Princeton, 1961.

Ashe, Robert P. *Two Kings of Uganda,* London, 1889.

Cook, Sir Albert R. *Uganda Memories (1897-1940),* Kampala, 1945.

Cook, G.C. 'Tribal Incidence of Lactose Deficiency in Uganda', *The Lancet,* April 2, 1966.

Crown Agents for the Colonies. *Notes for Officers appointed to Uganda,* London, 1934.

Cunningham, J.F. *Uganda and its People,* London, 1905.

Dahrendorf, Ralf. *Class and Class Conflict in Industrial Society,* London, 1959.

Doornbos, Martin R. 'Political Development: The Search for Criteria', *Development and Change,* I, 1, 1969-1970.

'Kumanyana and Rwenzururu: Two Responses to Ethnic Inequality', in Robert I. Rotberg and Ali A. Mazrui, (eds.) *Protest and Power in Black Africa,* New York, 1970.

'Protest Movements in Western Uganda: Some Parallels and Contrasts', *Kroniek van Afrika,* 1970, 3.

'Images and Reality of Stratification in Pre-colonial Nkore', *Canadian Journal of Africa Studies,* VII, 3, 1973.

Eaton, Joseph W. (ed.), *Institution Building and Development; From Concept to Application,* Beverly Hills and London, 1972.

Osman, Milton J. and Bruhns, Fred C. 'Institution Building in National Development: An Approach to Induced Social Change in Transitional Societies', in Hollis W. Peter, (ed.), *Comparative Theories of Social Change,* Ann Arbor, 1966.

Fallers, L. 'The Predicament of the Modern African Chief', *American Anthropologist,* LVII, 2, 1955.

Fortes, M. and Evans-Pritchard, E.E. (eds.) *African Political Systems,* London, 1940.

Gorju, P.J. *Entre le Victoria, l'Albert et l'Edouard,* Rennes, *1920.*

Heusch, Luc de. *Le Roi Ivre ou l'origine de l'Etat,* Paris, 1972.

Huntington, Samuel P. 'Political Development and Political Decay', *World Politics,* XVII, 3, 1965.

Political Order in Changing Societies, New Haven and London, 1968.
Johnston, Sir Harry. *The Uganda Protectorate, Vol I and II*, London, 1902.
Kabwegyere, Tarsis B. 'The Dynamics of Colonial Violence: The Inductive System in Uganda', *The Journal of Peace Research*, IX, 4, 1972.
Karugire, S.R. *A History of the Kingdom of Nkore in Western Uganda to 1896*, Oxford, 1971.
Katate, A.G. and Kamugungunu, L. *Abagabe b 'Ankole*, Ekitabo I and II, Kampala, 1955.
Kottak, Conrad P. 'Ecological Variables in the Origin and Evolution of African States: the Buganda Example', *Comparative Studies in Society and History*, XIV, 3, 1972.
Landau, E.R. *Political Systems of Highland Burma*, London, 1954.
Lemarchand, Rene. *Rwanda and Burundi*, London, 1961.
Lloyd, Peter C. 'The Political Structure of African Kingdoms: An Exploratory Model', in M. Banton, ed., *Political Systems and the Distribution of Power*, London, 1965.
Lowie, Robert H. *Social Organization*, London, 1950.
Lukyn Williams, F. 'The Inuguration of the Omugabe of Ankole to Office', *Uganda Journal*, IV, 4, 1937.
'Blood brotherhood in Ankole (Omukago)' *Uganda Journal*, II, 1, 1934.
'Nuwa Mbaguta, Nganzi of Ankole', *Uganda Journal*, X, 2, 1946.
Mackintosh, W.L.S. *Some notes on the Bahima and the Cattle Industry in Ankole*, Mbarara, 1938.
Maquet, Jacques J. *The Premise of Inequality*, London, 1961.
'Institutionalism Feodale des relations de dependence dans quatre cultures interlacustrines'. *Colloque du Groupe de Recherches en Anthropologice et Sociologie Politique*, Paris, 1968, (mimeo).
Mead, Margaret (ed.) *Cultural Patterns and Technical Change*, Paris, 1953.
'The Making of Ankole', *Uganda Journal*, XXI, 1, 1957.
'The Murder of H. St. Galt', *Uganda Journal*, XXIV, 1, 1960.
Morris, H.F. *A History of Ankole*, Kampala, 1962.
The Heroic Recitations of the Bahima of Ankole, Oxford, 1964.
Mungonya, Z.C.K. 'The Bacweziin Ankole', *Uganda Journal*, XXII, 1, 1958.
Mushanga, M.T. 'The Clan System among the Banyankore', *Uganda Journal*, XXXIV, 1, 1970.
Ntare School History Society. *The Governmental Institutions in Ankole before the British Rule*, mimeo, Mbarara, (n.d. 1965).
Nyerere, Julius K. *Freedom and Development*, Dar es Salaam, 1968.
Oberg, K. 'The Kingdom of Ankole in Uganda', in M. Fortes and E.E. Evans - Pritchard (eds.) *African Political Systems*, London, 1940.

Posnansky, Merrick. 'Kingship, Archeology and Historical Myth', *Uganda Journal*, XXX, 1, 1966.
Richards, Audrey, I. (ed.) *East African Chiefs*, London, 1959.
Roscoe, John. *The Banyankore*, Cambridge, 1923.
Sekanyolya. Luganda paper, Kampala.
Southwold, Martin. *Bureaucracy and Chiefship in Buganda*, East African Studies, No. 14, Kampala, 1961.
Speke, J.H. *Journal of the Discovery of the Source of the Nile*, London, 1863.
Stenning, D.J. 'Salvation in Ankole', in M. Fortes and G. Dieterlen, (eds.), *African Systems of Thought*, London, 1965.
'The Nyankole', in Audrey I. Richards, (ed.), *East African Music*, IV, 1.
Taylor, Brian K. *The Western Lacustrine Bantu*, London, 1962.
The People. Weekly, (changed later into a daily) paper Kampala.
Thiel, Paul van. 'The Music of the Kingdom of Ankole', *African Music*, IV, 1.
Tucker, Alfred R. *Eighteen Years in Uganda and East Africa*, London, 1911.
Uganda Argus. Daily paper, Kampala.
Uganda Government. *Constitution of Uganda*, 1962.
Constitution of the Republic of Uganda, 1967.
Statistical Abstract, 1971.
Uganda News. Ministry of Information and Broadcasting, Kampala, Uganda.
Uganda Protectorate. *Ankole Agreement*, 1901.
Native Administration, Entebbe, 1939.
Report on the Runyankore-Rukiga Orthographic Conference, Government Printer, 1956.
Uzoigwe, G.N. 'Pre-colonial Markets in Bunyoro-Kitara'. *Comparative Studies in Society and History*, XXIV, 4, 1972.
Vansina, J. 'A Comparison of African Kingdoms', *Africa* XXXII, 4, 1962.
Webster, J.B. (ed.) *Uganda Before 1900*, I, Nairobi, 1973.
Willis, J. *Willis Journal, Vol. I and II*, unpublished. (Makerere University Library).
Wrigley, C.C. 'Some Thoughts on the Bacwezi', *Uganda Journal*, XXII, 1, 1958.

Index

Abataremwa ba Rubambansi, 68
Abolition of Ankole kingship, 1-5, 74
Accession ceremonies, 65
Administrative officers, 3
Ankole agreement of 1901, 32, 37
Ankole agreement of 1962, 71
Ankole district, 6
Ankole district annual report, 48, 50
Ankole, expansion of, 34-36
Ankole government, 71
Annulment of the coronation of, 108
Armed forces of Uganda, 73

Babito ruling group 6
Bacwezi, 2, 7
Baganda chiefs, 54
Bahinda, 5, 6, 37, 38, 83
Bahima, 5, 11-24, 53-59
Bairu, 5, 11-24, 53-59
Bairu-Bahima division, 9-10, 53
Bagyendanwa, 2, 64, 67
Bakopi, 48
Bakururu clan, 67
Bantu, 7
Banyankore, 2, 3
Banyankore Cultural Foundation (BCF), 97, 114
Barigye, John (Prince), 96, 98
Bashambo, 37, 38, 39
Berlin Conference, 30
Bishop Stuart, 65
British Administration, 44
British monarchy, 75
British Officials, 43, 44, 50
Bukoba, 6
Buganda, 6, 70, 91, 93
Buganda crisis, 73
Buhaya, 6
Bunyoro, 6, 7, 68, 91, 93
Ceremonial forms of kingship, 91
Ceremonial robes, 65
Central bureaucratic structures, 9

Centralisation, 32
Clan membership, 8
Collector-colonial officer, 44, 45
Colonial administration, 54
Colonial officers, 44, 48
Constituent assembly, 91
Constitution of 1967, 3
Constitution of 1995, 105
Constitutional Commission, 105
Constitutional monarchy, 43, 69
Coronation anniversary, 65
Coronation chair, 63
Customary greeting, 67
Decentralisation, 94
Democratic Party (DP), 71, 72
District Commissioner, 32, 44, 46, 47, 48, 64
District Officials, 43
Economic goods, 8
Ebyaffe, 92, 93, 95
Eishengyero, 65, 67, 69
Enganzi, 37, 63, 64, 65, 71
European colonisation in Africa, 4
European colonialism - impact on
Historic Nkore system, 28-30
Ethnic divisions, 5
Ethnic status, 9
Federalism, 70, 94
Gasyonga - Omugabe of, 2, 49, 52, 65, 89
Government policy, 49
Governor, 48, 71
Idi Amin, 74, 87
Igumira, 38
Iguru, Solomon (Prince), 96
Independence constitution of Uganda, 1962, 71
Institutional decline, 75
Interlacustrine region, 6, 7, 8
Interstate relationships, 6
Kabaka, 70, 73, 91
Kabaka Yekka (KY), 71, 72, 73

140

Index

Kaboyo, Patrick, 91
Kahaya- Omugabe of, 39, 45-52
Karagwe, 6
Kategaya, Eriya, 111
Katikiro, 48
KY badges, 71, 72
Linguistic identity, 7
Local government reform, 69
Lukiiko, 46, 47, 91
Monarchial restoration bill, 94
Mugaba, 67
Museveni, Yoweri, 98
Mutesa, Edward (Sir), 87
Mythical charter, 7
National Resistance Council (NRC), 92
National Resistance Movement (NRM), 91, 98
Native Authority, 43
Native government, 48
Neo-traditionalisation, 74, 75
Nkore Cultural Trust (NCT), 97, 111, 113, 114
Nkore- kingdom of, 6
Nkore political system, 10
Ntare V, 7, 38
Nuwa Mbaguta, 37, 38, 39
Obote, 87
Obugabeship, 69, 70

Omugabe, 3, 13-24, 43-49
Omugabe-Ishe-Nyina-Bagyendanwa, 67
Omugabe wenka, 72
Omwigarire, 66
Poll tax, 49
Protectorate government, 63
Provincial Commissioner, 46, 47, 48, 49
Restoration of the Kabakaship, 88-89
Royal music, 68
Rubambansi the Omugabe, 69
Rukidi, John Mpuuga (Prince), 96
Rwanda, 6
Rwenzururu, 95
Seals of Ankole government, 67
Sekibobo, 48
Social basis of power, 5
Social mobility, 8, 10
Social organisation, 8
Sub-Commissioner, 44, 45
Subsistence- means of, 8, 11
Toro, 68, 91, 93, 95
Traditional authority, 4, 42, 43
Traditional rulers, 91, 94, 104
Traditional ruling class, 5
Uganda High Court, 72
Uganda Peoples Congress (UPC), 71, 72, 73

www.ingramcontent.com/pod-product-compliance
Lightning Source LLC
Chambersburg PA
CBHW070620300426
44113CB00010B/1604